THE FILMS OF
DAVID NIVEN

SERIES EDITOR: TOM HUTCHINSON

THE FILMS OF DAVID NIVEN

BY GERARD GARRETT

LSP BOOKS · LONDON

Acknowledgements

I would like to thank the many people whose help and cooperation made the production of this book possible. Principally among them were the charming, patient and industrious staff of the British Film Institute; Anglo-EMI; MGM-EMI; Fox-Rank; Cinema International Corporation; Columbia-Warner; HTV; The Kobal Collection; Four Star International Inc., Beverly Hills; and, of course, David Niven.

First published 1975 by
LSP BOOKS LIMITED
2 Denbigh Close, London W11 2QH
Copyright © 1975 by LSP BOOKS LIMITED
Printed in Great Britain by
Butler & Tanner Ltd., Frome and London
Designed by Jeff Tarry

ISBN 0 85321 066 7
ISBN 0 85321 069 1 (paperback)

FOREWORD

The world is currently being inundated with books on the cinema, and particularly about Hollywood, both in its earlier, formative days and its present. Indeed, I, too, have been invited by a publisher of previous good sense to prepare my own autobiography, and I am poised in the uncomfortable, if heady, position of having a great deal of work in hand and not enough time or energy to write both a book and a number of films, touch wood. Nevertheless, I am going to try very hard to join the throng of authors in the field, but I have no false illusions that my book will ever be as successful as David Niven's have been. Unquestionably, David is in the unique and enviable position of being the most successful author of a 'Hollywood' book ever, although, of course, his two autobiographical volumes have travelled a good distance away from the film capital. Indeed, David has been so successful in his avocation that there is very little about him that is not already known (and enjoyed) by almost anyone who can read.

I have only had the pleasure of working with him once, on my film *The Guns of Navarone*. David is, of course, a pleasure to work with, a producer and director's delight, supremely co-operative, always cheerful, always prepared, a ripplemaker of tremendous ingenuity, and, of course, one of the great raconteurs of all time. He is, moreover, a very brave man. I shall never forget how he literally dragged himself from a sick bed, barely recovered from a near-fatal blood disease, and insisted on completing a vital scene which, by holding up the completion of the film, was threatening a financial disaster to the distributors, Columbia Pictures. The consequences to David would have been more serious, as well as conclusive.

He has been most fortunate, I am happy to say, in Gerard Garrett's affection and admiration for him, and the result of those sentiments. I must say that I have never known a more complete filmography, and I am tremendously impressed by the fantastic job of research that has gone into it. I am not aware that it has any equal. It is, of course, simply another evidence of that quality which has made Gerard Garrett warmly liked by all of us who work in the cinema: we know how much he loves films and everything about them, and for that reason we always think of him as a friend, and not only as a critic or (as is often the case) a competitor. He knows our difficulties and our problems, he never takes advantage of them, he weighs them carefully in arriving at a balance of our achievements and failures, and he is always fair. This book is an example of that love for the cinema which has characterised him and his career, and I wish both him and the book extremely well.

CARL FOREMAN

To My Mother and Father

CONTENTS

INTRODUCTION

When David Niven presented himself for a job as a Hollywood extra in 1934, Central Casting, who supplied extras to the studios, registered him as Anglo-Saxon Type 2008 and gave him his first job — as a Mexican bandit, complete with drooping moustache, in a Western. You could consider this just one of the milder eccentricities of the old film capital. But in justice it must be remembered that about the only useful accomplishment the 24-year-old Niven could offer the film business was his ability to ride. Ironic, of course, that this distinctive feature of the British upper classes, of which Niven was a member, made common ground with the average American yokel. Needless to say he made numerous Westerns during his short career as an extra.

They were not his first experiences before the cameras. While a professional Army officer in Britain a friend put him up for a job while he was on leave as an extra in Sound City's comedy *All The Winners*. Fired by this experience Niven promptly applied for a part in Alexander Korda's projected epic *The Private Life of Henry VIII*, starring Charles Laughton and an illustrious cast, and destined to become one of Britain's great films. He was invited along by London Films, photographed, and finally sent on his way in a most uncivil manner.

As he nursed no burning ambition to become an actor, Niven shelved the film business as a potential career and, quite literally, soldiered on. While he was still an infant his father had been killed fighting the Turks in the first World War. His mother married again, to politician Sir Thomas Comyn-Platt, and young David was despatched to boarding school, then to Stowe and, having selected the Army as a career, to Sandhurst. He was accepted into the Highland Light Infantry and, judging by his own account, found life for a young lieutenant in the British army between the wars one long undergraduate jape. But it was unsatisfying enough for Niven to abandon it after only four years.

Thus he was thrust on the labour market with no particularly relevant qualifications to offer commercial employers. He had the benefit of his social status (which could, of course, also be limiting); the right connections, the old school tie network. In this milieu his standing was further enhanced by his charm (a word that was due to haunt his career), his natural friendliness and his capacity to entertain. He was an actor from the start even if his audience was a small and a select one. These were vital assets for he was also poor. The rich can forgive almost any vice among their own except poverty.

It is not surprising, with his adventurous disposition, that he should think of trying his hand in the New World, still a place of opportunity for young men, where his breeding would be no constraint and he could pursue any calling he fancied without embarrassment, certain to be considered by almost anyone as quite as good as themselves.

His attempts to make his fortune, first in Canada and then in New York, were marked mainly by their oddity and originality rather than by their success. Finally he made the crucial decision to embark for California to offer himself to Hollywood with little doubt in his mind that they would jump at the offer.

In Hollywood in those days theatrical training and acting experience were not necessary prerequisites but few future major stars could have arrived there with nothing but a handful of appearances in school and army concerts to their credit. Fewer still could have presented themselves with so scant a sense of vocation.

'This is a terrible confession to make,' he says. 'But after I left the Army I had a number of things to try. I had the great conceit to think that if all else failed I could always go to Hollywood. So when all else did fail I really went to Hollywood. And then I found out how wrong I was.'

After sorting out some initial problems, among them the fact that he did not possess the essential permit to work, he got himself employment as an extra: after a few abortive screen tests one optimistic agent put him up to the producer of a planned Western film

9

series as the possible star. On discovering he was English the producer despatched him from his office in an atmosphere of the kind of cordiality that must have prevailed at the gun fight at the O.K. Corral. The series was *Hopalong Cassidy*; William Boyd got the part and became the hero of a million Saturday morning children's matinées. David Niven did get into it a few times, as an extra.

He was an uncommon extra. He was friendly with the British Hollywood contingent of actors, Ronald Colman among them. He was on equally good terms with some useful Americans, including Loretta Young who gave a lot of help and encouragement. But these connections could not bridge that wide, wide gap between the Hollywood extra and the Hollywood actor. He was on the verge of giving up when he was able to jump that gap by a miraculous accident, one that occurred on account of the affable actor's endless network of friends in the right places. He became caught up, via a party aboard one of the ships of H.M.'s navy, in a publicity stunt on behalf of the first film version of *The Mutiny on the Bounty* and his name stuck in the mind of the producer, and Hollywood founding father, Irving Thalberg.

Thalberg thought it might be a further neat publicity gimmick to give Niven a tiny part in the film. The moment the news leaked out that Thalberg wanted Niven other famous noses got the scent. Sam Goldwyn, not to be outdone by a rival, snapped up the astonished Niven and signed him up for seven years.

It was the sort of dramatic success story Hollywood likes to circulate. In Niven's account his agent had to give Goldwyn something of the hard sell before the deal was made. It is likely that the astute Goldwyn was not entirely unaware of Niven's existence, as he had made such an agreeable impression around town and was, in addition, a friend of another of his contract stars, Ronald Colman. But it was for Niven, in any event, a remarkable reversal of fortune and the real beginning of a long, brilliant and unbroken career.

The ballyhoo began and news of Sam's latest discovery was fed to the world Press. His debut was to be in *Dark Victory* with Merle Oberon, a lady with whom he was subsequently linked romantically. It didn't happen and his first job turned out to be a walk-across screen part in *Without Regret* with Elissa Landi and Paul Cavanaugh—not for Goldwyn, but as a loan-out to Paramount.

The loan-out system was a sore point with most stars and a constant cause of friction between actors and studio, and Niven, in time, grew very irritated with it. In brief, it meant that the studio hired players at one price and then rented them out at a profit. It was not entirely a one-way traffic: occa-

sionally the actor got a better part as a result of the system than he might have had from his own studio; sometimes, of course, he got a worse one.

His second film was a Goldwyn production, *Barbary Coast*, a star-studded, first feature in which he uttered his first line of dialogue.

Only one of his next five pictures was for Goldwyn but the period was notable for his first film as one of the leads, a B-picture version of *Thank You, Jeeves* in which, naturally, he played Bertie Wooster and made a remarkably good job of it. It was an event that revealed Niven as a man with a future and producers should have taken more account of it than they did.

He returned to Goldwyn for a really major feature, *Dodsworth*, down the cast list again and in an unimpressive part.

But he was working regularly and progressing steadily. He was worth noticing in *The Prisoner of Zenda*, registered well in a brief part of no great account in *Bluebeard's Eighth Wife* and scored a positive hit in *The Dawn Patrol*.

He reached the fourth year of his contract with his

One of the actor's minor chores, plugging the finished picture. David Niven with Douglas Fairbanks Jnr., Madeleine Carroll, Ronald Colman and bluff C. Aubrey Smith on the Lux radio show on behalf of *The Prisoner of Zenda*.

reputation rising nicely, partly through the industry of Goldwyn's head of publicity Jock Lawrence and also by his ability to shine, often from dark corners, in films that were good, and to appear patently blameless in films that were bad.

But then came three pictures that displayed in their different ways the essential characteristics of Niven the actor and are reflected in most of the parts he would undertake in the future.

Edgar Linton in *Wuthering Heights* is the sort of rôle that actors with an eye to their fan rating leave town to avoid. Niven did his best to get out of it but Goldwyn, fortunately, was adamant. Instead of the weak and handsome ninny we might have expected, Niven turned Linton into a character who earned and held our sympathy to the end despite his limpness. In his autobiography the actor celebrates the shooting of the film with a tasteless anecdote which would be lamentable, were it not so obviously a typical Niven device for steering our attention away from any close consideration of the craftsmanship and sensitivity that went into building one of his characterisations.

His capacity to make acceptable and even attractive the sort of man outwardly admirable, but inwardly a soft and sagging reed, was frequently exploited by producers (Major Burnside in *Before Winter Comes* for instance) and reached its nadir (through no fault of the actor) in *Eye of the Devil* in 1966 when Phillipe de Montfaucon dutifully sacrifices himself as part of some dotty family destiny.

Bachelor Mother with Ginger Rogers fully established Niven's brilliance in light comedy in the grand tradition of such names as Melvyn Douglas, William Powell, Cary Grant and Rex Harrison. It was not his best comedy performance—there were many at least as good to come—but it was undoubtedly the best comedy script he has ever had.

Raffles, to complete the hat trick, showed him as the witty bounder and the charming adventurer, and he was to play the part in many guises in future films and in his TV series *The Rogues*. Raffles was not a great hit with the critics, but a coin-rattling success at the box office.

His career was hot and it was time to strike out for a better deal, but this was 1939 and the next dramatic event in his life was the outbreak of war and the need he felt to return to Britain and join in the fighting.

He was released from the Army to make two British films geared to the times, but it was over five years before he could get back to Hollywood. When he arrived Sam Goldwyn led other producers in offering the big hand but none of them had much for him up their sleeves.

The pictures he was offered were a bleak lot and, after completing a film with Shirley Temple of incredible silliness (another of those frequent loan-outs), he finally asked Sam Goldwyn to release him from his contract. Their relationship had its ups and downs but the parting seemed amicable enough until Goldwyn wickedly announced to the world he'd given Niven the sack, which was not the best note on which to start a new career as a free-lance actor in the film capital where the movie moguls, even if their power was waning, were still in effective control.

Goldwyn could be an implacable enemy but he clearly had a soft spot for Niven and a photograph of the actor remained displayed on his piano until the end.

Niven moved out into an unfriendly world, his reputation groggy from a succession of bad pictures, and if he felt that he could hardly do worse on his own account, he was to be proved sadly wrong. He could and did.

His first independent deals took him into a supporting role to Mario Lanza in some vocal gush called *The Toast of New Orleans* and into an imitation American musical made in Britain called *Happy-Go-Lovely*.

Times are rarely bad enough that the cheery Niven cannot look back and find a light side. In the case of *The Toast of New Orleans* he recalls the fact that Mario Lanza had an obsessive regard for Caruso. Caruso had bladder trouble and as a result kept a suitable receptacle in his dressing room. Lanza, it seems, did the same.

Each morning Niven found the foully foaming pot deposited outside his door. This nuisance was only abated when he demanded time off from producer Joe Pasternak to have an innoculation against typhoid.

From then on it was mainly downhill until it was generally considered that his career as a Hollywood star was all but finished.

The perceptive Otto Preminger, against establishment advice, put him into *The Moon Is Blue* and if

Another chore, keeping in the public eye. Niven sits behind Claudette Colbert at the first night of a Hollywood ice revue in 1938.

With first wife Primmie and David Jnr. who became a film executive.

Dutiful smiles he didn't feel summoned up for Sam Goldwyn's publicity photographer and sons David and Jamie at his Hollywood home. The time: shortly after Primmie's tragic death.

Sharing a table with Rita Hayworth, producer Harold Hecht and Deborah Kerr while filming *Separate Tables*.

With Mario Lanza and Howard Keel at MGM.

It's a sentimental world but never mixes its sentiment with business. David Niven may have been one of the most popular men around but when it came to a part he had no better chance than the next person.

His popularity has become a legend, so much so that there is almost an urge to puncture it. In no mean spirit, but strictly in the interests of fact, I tried to discover somebody who knew or worked with him who might have a harsh word to say of him. I could find no one.

The show business reporter of one of our brasher newspapers, calloused by collisions with countless star performers, met Niven for the first time at a reception to launch his film *Paper Tiger*. He told me:

'I was determined to find out if the man was as nice as everybody says he was—and he is.'

He has, of course, a few detractors. Lofty commentators on the film scene like to cast him as a handy representative figure of the successful, commercial cinema to be brought out now and again as a whipping boy and scourged in print. More reasonable people take no such view but were, perhaps, sometimes unfavourably influenced by what we could call the 'Trubshawe Syndrome'.

Trubshawe was Niven's bluff soldier friend with the looks of a country squire who took up acting

With Doris Day.

With Hjordis, his Swedish-born second wife. (Below) visiting Deborah Kerr at the Paramount studio.

and was adopted by the Press as a 'colourful character' and became a sort of embodiment, possibly unjustly, of that jokey, raucous hunting, shooting and fishing world that seemed a part of the Niven scene. The blood sports aspect (odd in a man as kindly as Niven) may not have adversely affected critics on humanitarian grounds, for they could be savage enough when in pursuit of an offending actor or actress, but as our hunting, shooting and fishing fraternity hardly represent the more aesthetic aspect of society Niven's identification with it did not particularly enhance his prestige as a serious actor.

Keeping Hedda Hopper happy . . . Hollywood's most assiduous gossip gatherer.

As I have suggested he didn't improve his image as a dedicated artist either by his apparently frivolous attitude to his career even though, as I believe, this stemmed only from an acute sense of modesty.

Such matters may not have loomed large in the mind of the general public, who seemed to adore him in any guise, but in the over-publicised and over-heated atmosphere of the film business such details go a long way in deciding wary film reviewers whom among the stars to treat with respect and whom with gentle scorn.

Too many people, including too many producers and quite a few critics, took him at his face value as a genial fellow swanning through his parts, being himself, and delighting in getting paid for having such fun.

His capacity for coping with the worst of the material the film business could find for him occasionally breaks down: the result is revealing. Immobility seems to set in, the strain shows and a sort of paralysis of invention is evident. It is at these moments that his skill, remembered from other films, is thrown into relief. He is an actor of a purity of style in which the inner conflicts don't break the

21

Posing in the rain with William Holden. Location, Britain, naturally.

surface, and unlike some of his colleagues he relies little on mannerisms and tricks.

It is hard to believe that actors of this era as varied as Ronald Colman, Humphrey Bogart, Clark Gable, Cary Grant, Gary Cooper and even Spencer Tracy would have held their place for so long on the sort of material consistently doled out to Niven. And yet all these illustrious names have been seen in more poor films than they have ever appeared in good ones. It could be said that the famous film actor is always greater than the sum of his parts. For David Niven the opposite seems to have applied, perhaps

because he has had far too few films that have scored as major successes in every department.

Nevertheless his popularity with audiences—like the faith of many producers—has never seriously wavered. He has the blessed gift, variously described as loved by the camera, generating electricity or comprising exactly the right chemistry, of holding the massive film and television audiences of the world for over 40 years.

Like most leading men in Hollywood he has been required to make the fullest romantic impact upon women and has developed an approach all his own.

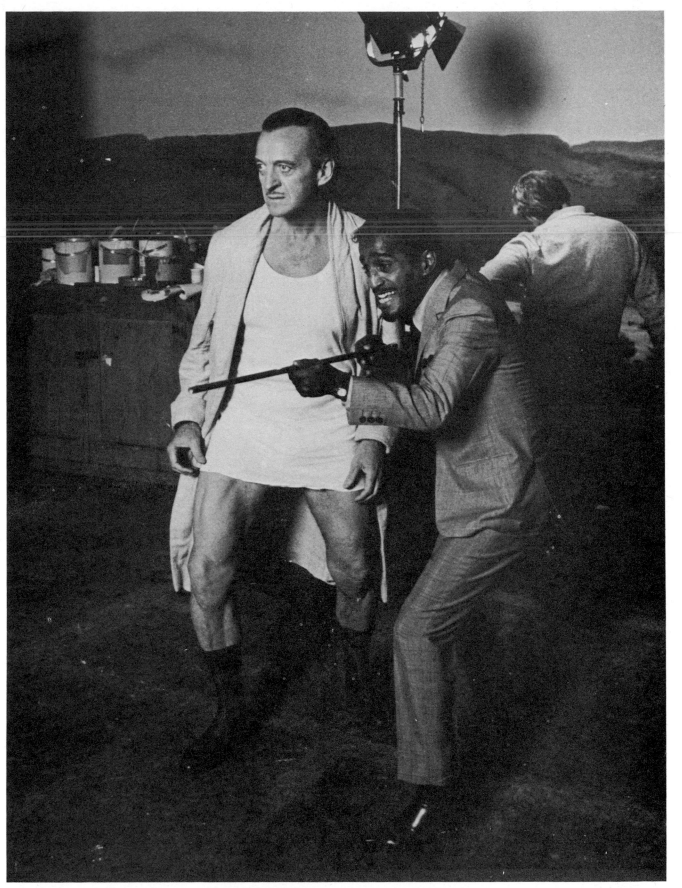

Sammy Davis Jnr. visits the set of *Casino Royale.*

It is difficult for a male to analyse what precisely his effect in this department has been; his best comedy parts and many of his serious ones have been characterised by a certain helplessness which he has the skill to project in a captivating manner. I would not say women have always viewed him without more powerful passions, but I would guess that the desire to offer reassurance has been a consistent factor.

Niven himself would never publicly probe so deeply into any of the elements that have formulated his artistry or created his appeal. His sort of background precludes it: you do not give yourself airs and graces, over-estimate your own importance or parade your heart on your sleeve at Stowe and Sandhurst. A soldier is trained to camouflage more than material objects. It makes Niven an uncharacteristic actor, but still a memorable one.

With adopted daughters Krinstina
and Fiona and wife Hjordis.

FILMOGRAPHY

One of David Niven's earliest recollections of life before the Hollywood cameras was as an extra appearing as a half-naked slave, lashed with 'hurt-proof whips', in a Cecil B. DeMille epic. He thinks it was *Cleopatra* (the one starring Claudette Colbert) and he could be right, as it was in production at Paramount in 1934 when the actor was doing his few months' stint in the crowd before Sam Goldwyn offered him a contract in the June of that year.

There was not much glamour in the life of an extra, nor had they much identity with the films in which they appeared. 'In those days you took your two dollars and never asked what picture you were in,' Niven says. 'I know I was in a Marie Dressler film once because I saw her on the set.'

He was an extra in a number of M.G.M. pictures, mainly in Westerns. 'I was always in the beastly posse.'

He was accidently involved in a publicity stunt for the Clark Gable–Charles Laughton *The Mutiny on the Bounty* but not in the film. Mae West briefly considered him as a potential leading man.

Niven's activity in the theatre has been negligible. He appeared in New York in *Nina* with Gloria Swanson shortly after his parting with Goldwyn and with his career situation rather sticky. Preminger saw him in the play, which was otherwise a disaster for everyone concerned, and booked him for his film version of *The Moon is Blue*. At Preminger's request he acted in the play for three months in San Francisco before appearing in the film.

He's had a heavy involvement with TV. Rather daringly he teamed up with Dick Powell and Charles Boyer to form Four Star Playhouse to make TV films at a time when Hollywood viewed TV as its greatest single enemy.

Dick Powell was the business brains, David Niven the publicity expert. The business boomed and began the uneasy rapport between TV and the motion

As *The Canterville Ghost.*

picture business. Niven, still out of favour in Hollywood, could afford to risk the wrath of the studio heads. But it was not such a risk after all. As he told me, the movie moguls respected successful show-business gambles. When Dick Powell died the fortunes of the company waned. Niven held on to some shares but it was bought by a Texas concern and became mainly concerned with film distribution.

In 1973 he came to Britain to make an Anglo-American TV co-production of a dramatisation of Oscar Wilde's *The Canterville Ghost* at the studios of HTV, the Wales and the West Country Commercial TV regional company.

In 1961 he had joined the list of the Hollywood mighty who had made guest appearances in the *Road* films.

This one was *Road to Hong Kong* as usual written, directed and produced by the team of Norman Panama and Melvin Frank. Bob Hope and Bing Crosby were joined by Joan Collins, and the star duo's old girl friend Dorothy Lamour made a courtesy appearance. It was over 20 years since the production of the first *Road* film and this one turned out to be a pallid exercise in nostalgia with Niven's split-second appearance as a Tibetan monk going for very little.

His fame, like so many Hollywood stars, is based soundly on the cinema. In one other area only has he secured comparable success: and that has been as an author.

His chapters of autobiography *The Moon's A Balloon* was a runaway, world-wide best seller. But he began writing in 1951 with a novel called *Round The Ragged Rocks*. If its reception hardly matched the triumph of *The Moon's A Balloon* it had a very respectable success selling over 20,000 copies in America and about 12,000 in Britain.

Niven resisted pressure to re-publish the book in the light of later literary success. It was based on incidents in his life, although a fictional work, and some of those incidents, in their actual settings, re-appeared in *The Moon's A Balloon.*

Bring on the Empty Horses, his third book, is devoted to his famous contemporaries and many minor figures as well. The enigmatic title sprang from a typical Niven film-making experience. When he was in *The Charge of the Light Brigade* with Errol Flynn, Michael Curtiz, a director whose grasp of the English language was fragile indeed, ordered that the riderless steeds should be driven across the set with the phrase: 'Bring on the empty horses.'

When he spotted Flynn and Niven shaking with merry laughter he cursed them furiously through his megaphone, ending his tirades of fractured oaths with one of the most famous, but rarely printed, of all Hollywood howlers.

'You think I know f—— nothing—and I know f—— all.'

Grim jesting for Anglo-American TV version of Oscar Wilde's story.

28

WITHOUT REGRET

1935

Paramount. *Producer*: B. P. Fineman. *Director*: Harold Young. *Script*: Doris Anderson, Charles Brackett. *Camera*: William C. Mellor. *Running time*: 74 minutes.

CAST

Elissa Landi . . . . *Jennifer Gage*
Paul Cavanagh . . . . *Robert Godfrey*
Frances Drake . . . . *Mona Gould*
Kent Taylor . . . . *Steven Paradin*
Gilbert Emery . . . . *Inspector Hayes*
David Niven . . . . *Bill Gage*
Peter H. Hobbes . . . . *Fred*
Reginald Sheffield . . . . *Reporter*
Forrester Harvey . . . . *Police Surgeon*
Betty Holt . . . . *Jennifer's Child*

STORY

Something awkward happens to Jennifer Gage while travelling in China: she is seized by bandits. Steven Paradin, an airman employed by the bandits, helps her, woos her and marries her, abandoning Mona Gould, till then his sweetheart, in the process.
Some years later Jennifer, conveniently rescued from what turned out to be an unfortunate adventure by the death of Steven in a plane crash, is happily married to successful heart specialist Robert Godfrey, in London.
Discarded Mona appears on the scene and so does Steven, who survived after all. Steven's feelings for Jennifer still flicker and Mona knows it. She tries to blackmail Jennifer. Intrigue and murder follow. Steven poisons Mona but it's Jennifer who is suspected by Inspector Hayes of the Yard. Steven does the decent thing, confesses, and leaves Robert and Jennifer to their happiness.

NOTES

Seriously subdued, considering Hollywood ballyhoo was at its prime, the Paramount publicity department contented themselves with describing this picture as just A Powerful Drama. It certainly didn't send out many ripples in the Hollywood pond but must remain enshrined in the hearts of all Niven's admirers as the first film in which he was elevated from the ranks and actually spoke.
He occupied a healthy position on the cast list too, a concession to the publicity value of his recently acquired Goldwyn contract. But his major dramatic activity was delivering a single consoling line to heroine Elissa Landi—an actress rarely remembered but who was the Grace Kelly of her day.

Without Regret provided picturegoers with a gracious heroine (here in trouble in China), a dusty plot and a fleeting glimpse of David Niven as a fully-fledged actor.

BARBARY COAST

1935

A Samuel Goldwyn Production. *Producer*: Sam Goldwyn. *Director*: Howard Hawkes. *Script*: Ray June —*from an original by* Ben Hecht and Charles MacArthur. *Camera*: Edward Curtis. *Running time*: 97 minutes.

CAST

Miriam Hopkins	*Melissa Swan*
Edward G. Robinson	*Chamalis*
Joel McCrea	*Carmichael*
Walter Brennan	*Old Atrocity*
Frank Craven	*Colonel Cobb*
Brian Donlevy	*Knuckles*
Harry Carey	*Slocum*
J. M. Kerrigan	*Judge Harper*
Donald Meek	*McTavish*
David Niven	*Sailor*

STORY

Melissa Swan, a nice, clean girl from the East Coast, ventures unsuspectingly into the waterfront area of San Francisco while it is going lawlessly wild during the great gold rush of 1850.

The man she has come to marry turns up dead, a casualty of the gang wars. Penniless, she sinks into vice and into the hands of the top racketeer, becoming the most notorious floozy on the Barbary coast, also a dab hand at gulling the guileless in gambling hell-holes.

Carmichael, a decent prospector, falls for Melissa while being fleeced. He redeems her through love and the chief bad man receives his just deserts at the hands of a band of vigilantes.

NOTES

Having discreetly tried out Niven by loaning him out for *Without Regret,* Sam Goldwyn now popped his latest discovery into a one-liner part as a cockney sailor in this colourful, star-studded adventure extravaganza which managed to suggest something of the real vice-ridden haunts of San Francisco of the period without offending the censor's office.

In the billing Niven was able to rub shoulders with Donald Meek, that crumpled little teddy bear of a man and one of the most effective bit players Hollywood ever discovered.

Niven's one line of dialogue was lost in the general hubbub and dramatically his brief high spot was being thrown out of the window of a San Francisco brothel during a riot. He had arrived, at any rate, where the action was.

The *New York Times* found the picture 'a merry, vigorous and delectably phrased tale of blood and passion'.

Miriam Hopkins and Edward G. Robinson in *Barbary Coast.*

A FEATHER IN HER HAT

1935

Columbia. *Producer*: Everett Riskin. *Director*: Alfred Santell. *Script*: Lawrence Hazard—*from a story by* I. Wylie. *Camera*: Joseph Walker. *Editor*: Viola Lawrence. *Running time*: 70 minutes.

CAST

Pauline Lord . . . . *Clarissa Phipps*
Basil Rathbone . . . . *Captain Courtney*
Louis Hayward . . . . *Richard Orland*
Billie Burke . . . . *Julia Trent Anders*
Wendy Barrie. . . . . *Pauline Anders*
Victor Varconi . . . . *Paul Anders*
Nydia Westman . . . . *Emily Judson*
Thurston Hall . . . . *Sir Elroyd Joyce*
Nana Bryant . . . . *Lady Drake*
J. M. Kerrigan . . . . *Pobjay*
Doris Lloyd . . . . *Liz Vanning*
David Niven . . . . *Leo Cartwright*
John Rogers . . . . *Henry Vining*

STORY

Clarissa Phipps, the impoverished owner of an East End bookshop, is dedicated to the future of her love child, Richard. She provides a home for gallant Captain Courtney (alas, also a drunk) so that he can finance the boy's education.

When Richard is 21, Clarissa reveals to him the truth of his birth; he is not her son but the child of a famous actress who must remain nameless. With money provided by this lady, Richard is enabled to begin a literary career. Through a chance discovery of some letters Richard believes his mother is retired actress Julia Trent. He writes a play around her, which is accepted by the big impresario of the day and proves the hit of the season.

This success is too much for Clarissa who promptly expires, but not before confessing that *she* was the real mother, it was *her* hard-earned savings that launched his literary career and that she has fulfilled her life-time's ambition to turn him into a real gentleman of letters.

NOTES

This sickly sob story ('A shy and fragile little drama of mother love strives with minor success to make itself heard above the clatter of the plot', said the *New York Times* kindly) is mainly important in the Niven canon for providing him with his first big scene, at a literary party, in his role of Leo, the witty poet.

The actor recounts in *The Moon's A Balloon* how director Alfred Santell conspired to get him through the ordeal. He secretly arranged for all on the set to applaud the actor enthusiastically on his first take however bad he was—and Niven was pretty bad. On the second take the actor sailed through admirably with perfect confidence. Alfred Santell, naturally, is fondly remembered.

Louis Hayward, Pauline Lord and Basil Rathbone in *A Feather In Her Hat.*

SPLENDOUR

1935

Samuel Goldwyn Inc. *Producer:* Sam Goldwyn. *Director:* Elliot Nugent. *Script:* Rachel Crothers. *Camera:* Gregg Toland. *Editor:* Margaret Clancey. *Art director:* Richard Day. *Costume:* Omar Klam. *Sound:* Frank Maher. *Running time:* 77 minutes.

CAST

Miriam Hopkins	*Phylis Lorrimore*
Joel McCrea	*Brighton Lorrimore*
Paul Cavanagh	*Martin Deering*
Helen Westley	*Mrs. Lorrimore*
Billie Burke	*Clarissa*
Katherine Alexander	*Martha Lorrimore*
Ruth Weston	*Edith Gilbert*
David Niven	*Clancey Lorrimore*
Ivan Simpson	*Fletcher*
Arthur Treacher	*Captain Ballinger*

STORY

Matriachal Mrs Lorrimore, head of the Lorrimore clan, once wealthy, now in decline, schemes to save the family fortunes by organising a profitable marriage. Wastrel younger grandson Clancey is happy to marry multi-million dollar heiress Edith, dangled before his eyes, but she rejects him and elder grandson Brighton Lorrimore marries Phylis, beautiful but broke.

Mrs. Lorrimore plucks up hope when wealthy cousin Martin Deering arrives on the scene and fancies Phylis. Martin showers success on Brighton but Phylis's favours are the price and, encouraged by Mrs. Lorrimore, she pays it.

Clancey, going steadily from bad to worse, pesters Phylis for money and threatens to reveal her indiscretions if he doesn't get it.

Phylis chooses to confess to her husband. They part. Eventually Brighton contemptuously casts aside wealth, seeks out Phylis, now working in a cafeteria, and together they settle for life at the bottom of the ladder.

NOTES

This was one of Sam Goldwyn's cheeky films that—in the midst of a Hollywood letching and luxuriating—lectured the Depression era masses on the values of marital fidelity and genteel poverty.

It offered Niven his first character to play an integral part in the plot. But what a plot. And as a handsome wastrel, a failure in love and a flop as a crook, the Niven qualities hardly flourished.

Miriam Hopkins attracted the critical attention. *The Times* wrote: 'Without Miriam Hopkins *Splendour* would be a feeble enough affair'.

The *New York Times* considered the picture 'a model of dramatic exposition but that it suffers from inaction and its theme is too commonplace' and noted 'the unpleasant Lorrimores are acted with poisonous effectiveness by Helen Westley ... Katherine Alexander ... and David Niven as the useless son'.

Joel McCrea and Paul Cavanagh (right) are the leading men in *Splendour* but David Niven, looking disconsolate, is beginning to edge his way into the picture.

ROSE MARIE

1936

M.G.M. *Producer*: Hunt Stromberg. *Director*: W. S. Van Dyke. *Script*: Frances Goodrich, Albert Hackett, Alice Duer Miller—*from the book of the musical by* Otto A. Harbach and Oscar Hammerstein II. *Music*: Rudolf Friml, Herbert Stothart. *Camera*: William Daniels. *Editor*: Blanche Sewell. *Running time*: 110 minutes.

CAST

Jeanette MacDonald . . . . *Marie De Flor*
Nelson Eddy . . . . *Sergeant Bruce*
Reginald Owen . . . . *Myerson*
Allan Jones . . . . *Romeo*
James Stewart . . . . *John Flower*
Alan Mowbray . . . . *Premier*
David Niven . . . . *Teddy*
Herman Bing . . . . *Mr. Daniells*

STORY

Marie, the famous prima donna, displays her top notes and her tantrums but conceals a guilty secret. Her brother is a gaol-bird. When he escapes and flees to the Canadian rockies she throws up her career and hurries to help him. Coming to grief in the mountains Sergeant Bruce, a Canadian mountie, helps her. Romance blossoms. But duty comes first and Bruce insists on getting his man, Marie's brother. Romance founders.

Marie returns to Montreal and her career in opera. But when bits of the Indian Love Call keep getting hopelessly mixed up with Puccini in the last act of *Tosca*, Marie realises that she and her redcoat can never be apart and, in a trill, they are together again.

NOTES

This M.G.M. musical provided Niven with a melodious background but nothing much to sing about—this was really back to the chorus with his minute part as a wealthy playboy pursuing the prima donna whose attentions she throws off with the ease she tosses off a high C. David Niven, understandably, looks distinctly hang-dog during his brief appearance on screen.

The film was mainly remarkable for potting Gounod's five act opera *Romeo and Juliet* into about as many minutes, and as an example of Hollywood's hair-raising attitude to the serious music world. But it was a huge success and probably displayed Niven before

Famous Nelson Eddy—Jeanette MacDonald vocal battle. Niven merely one of the casualties.

a larger audience than all his previous films put together. Rave notices greeted the appearance of a new young actor. His name was James Stewart.

But, as the *New York Times* pointed out, 'Since this is Miss Macdonald's and Mr. Eddy's picture there can be no important place for other members of the cast...'

PALM SPRINGS

(U.S. Title: PALM SPRINGS AFFAIR)

1936

Paramount. *Producer*: Walter Wanger. *Director*: Aubrey Scotto. *Script*: Joseph Fields. *Musical director*: Boris Morros. *Camera*: James Van Trees. *Running time*: 72 minutes.

CAST

Frances Langford . . . . *Joan Smythe*
Sir Guy Standing . . . . *Major Smythe*
Ernest Cossart . . . . *Starkey*
Smith Ballew . . . . *Slim*
Spring Byington . . . . *Aunt Letty*
David Niven . . . . *George Brittel*
E. E. Clive . . . . *Bruce Morgan*
Sterling Holloway . . . . *Oscar*
Grady Sutton . . . . *Bud*

STORY

Impecunious Major Smythe and his butler Starkey take refuge in Palm Springs from their creditors. Daughter Joan, expelled from High School for gambling, comes to join them. She meets up with Slim, a handsome cowboy, and George Brittel, an ineffectual millionaire under the thumb of his Aunt Letty—but finds no trace of her father or Starkey.
She later discovers them working as croupiers. She decides to rescue both from this humiliating fate by marrying a millionaire, despite the fact she is falling in love with Slim. She picks on handy George Brittel. After a familiar spate of romantic machinations and complications Joan realises she loves Slim more than she loves duty (or George).

NOTES

This routine romantic musical did not mark any great improvement in the standard of picture Hollywood was dishing out to Niven at this time: but it did give him a comedy and it did cast him in a debonair role that foreshadowed things to come.
Kine Weekly, at least, greeted the film with some glee. 'The naïveté of this picture is both its charm and strength. So delightfully irresponsible is the treatment, and so kindly and infectiously humorous the major characterisations, that the orthodox is invested with a wealth of popular light entertainment.'

Impeccable in dinner jacket . . .

. . . and dashing in riding gear as a rather witless millionaire playboy in *Palm Springs.*

THANK YOU, JEEVES

1936

20th-Century Fox. *Producer:* Sol M. Wurtzel. *Director:* Arthur Greville Collins. *Script:* Joseph Hoffman, Stephen Gross—*after* P. G. Wodehouse. *Camera:* Barney McGill. *Editor:* Nick DeMaggio. *Running time:* 57 minutes.

CAST
Arthur Treacher . . . . *Jeeves*
Virginia Fields . . . . *Marjorie*
David Niven . . . . *Bertie Wooster*
Lester Matthews . . . . *Elliot Manville*
Collin Tapley . . . . *Tom Brock*

STORY
Bertie Wooster and Jeeves, his butler, are occupied with their usual ineffable affairs (suitable socks to go with the suiting, plans for lunch) when their decorous world is invaded by Marjorie, a mysterious charmer pursued by gunmen intent on grabbing an important document she has.

A Wooster is hardly likely to ignore a damsel in distress and consequently Bertie and Jeeves become involved in a great deal of comic skulduggery including complications with secret panels, a send-up punch-up and a Keystone Cop-style car chase before Bertie (but mainly Jeeves) saves the girl from the cads.

NOTES
In presenting Bertie Wooster and Jeeves on the screen one suspects that producer Sol M. Wurtzel (surely he must have stepped from a P. G. Wodehouse novel?) felt that while a little of its peculiarly British humour would go some of the way it would need bolstering up with plenty of Hollywood knockabout farce to complete the journey.

Certainly much of the action would cause raised eyebrows among the more athletic members of the Drones Club.

It was a mere B picture but it was a land-mark in the Niven career. Removed from gathering dust at the bottom of the credits, he was elevated to the stars. And he had a part tailor-made for him as Bertie Wooster.

He was able to demonstrate all his latent comic possibilities: those wide-eyed expressions of impending horror, those beguiling looks of perplexity, his capacity for exhaling the sort of charm that makes any upper-class nit-wit an object of elegance and delight.

Arthur Treacher—with Eric Blore Hollywood's definitive gentleman's gentleman—was admirable as Jeeves and the picture must be accounted an example of remarkably inspired casting.

Frank S. Nugent put it very nicely in the *New York Times*: 'Mr. Wodehouse must have been one of the fates in attendance at their [David Niven and Arthur Treacher] births, marking them to play the characters he has been writing about these many years.'

The big breakthrough. As Bertie Wooster with the inimitable Arther Treacher as Jeeves and Virginia Fields as the heroine.

DODSWORTH

1936

Samuel Goldwyn Inc. *Producer:* Sam Goldwyn. *Director:* William Wyler. *Script:* Sidney Howard—*from the novel by* Sinclair Lewis. *Camera:* Rudolph Mate. *Art:* Richard Day. *Editor:* Daniel Mandell. *Running time:* 108 minutes.

CAST

Walter Huston . . . . *Samuel Dodsworth*
Ruth Chatterton . . . . . *Fran Dodsworth*
Paul Lukas . . . . *Arnold Iselin*
Mary Astor . . . . *Edith Cortright*
David Niven . . . . *Major Lockert*
Gregory Gaye . . . . *Kurt von Obersdorf*
Maria Ouspenskaya . . . . *Baroness von Obersdorf*
Odette Myrtil . . . . *Madame de Penable*
Kathryn Marlowe . . . . . *Emily McKee*

STORY

Sam Dodsworth, a motor tycoon, and his wife Fran see their daughter Emily safely married and set off to do Europe. A shipboard flirtation with Major Lockert, a suave Englishman, quite turns Fran's head and transforms the trip into an escape route back to youth.

Believing herself desirable again she persuades Sam to halt the trip in Paris and there she falls for Arnold Iselin, another smoothie.

Cast-off, Sam leaves her to it but back home in America finds he still loves her. His return to Europe and an attempt at reconciliation fails. Since Fran has now become a grandmother, and Sam's presence reminds her of the fact, she likes him around even less and demands a divorce so that she can marry her latest passion, Kurt von Obersdorf, a young Austrian.

Fran's dream world soon collapses and she tries to get Sam back. In the meantime he has fallen for an understanding American divorcée, Mrs. Cortright, and has no desire to return to a frenetic life with Fran.

NOTES

This was one of those literary exercises (based on Sinclair Lewis's novel) that Hollywood liked to turn out at regular intervals, solidly carpentered and a trifle solemn. This one provided Niven with a chance to work with the masterly William Wyler, but in a part that was no more than another cog in the machine. It won an Academy Award for the art direction and provided a *tour-de-force* for Walter Huston. The *New York Times* liked the picture, considered Niven excellent in his tiny part and summed up: 'William Wyler . . . has had the skill to execute it in cinematic terms, and a gifted cast has been able to bring the whole alive to our complete satisfaction.'

David Niven modestly remarks that the film was a big hit 'in spite of my wooden performance'. A review of the film in the *Detroit Free Press* is the only one he has ever kept. It reads: 'In this picture we were privileged to see the great Samuel Goldwyn's latest discovery—all we can say about this actor (?) is that he is tall, dark and not the slightest bit handsome.'

In *Dodsworth* he was as an English military man with a ruthless way with the women.

Ruth Chatterton falls victim to his charms and has good cause to regret the fact.

THE CHARGE OF THE LIGHT BRIGADE

1936

Warner Brothers. *Producer*: Hal B. Wallis. *Director*: Michael Curtiz. *Script*: Michael Jacoby, Rowland Leigh—*'inspiration' from Tennyson's poem*. *Camera*: Sol Polito, Fred Jackman. *Music*: Max Steiner. *Art*: Jack Hughes. *Musical director*: Leo P. Forbstein. *Editor*: George Amy. *Running Time*: 116 minutes.

CAST

Errol Flynn . . . . *Major Geoffrey Vickers*
Olivia de Havilland . . . . *Elsa Campbell*
Patric Knowles . . . . . . *Captain Perry Vickers*
Henry Stephenson . . . . *Sir Charles Macefield*
Nigel Bruce . . . . *Sir Benjamin Warrenton*
Donald Crisp . . . . *Colonel Campbell*
David Niven . . . . *Captain Randall*
C. Henry Gordon . . . . . *Surat Khan*
G. P. Huntley Jnr. . . . . . *Major Jowett*
Robert Barrett . . . . . . *Count Igor Volonoff*
Spring Byington . . . . . . *Lady Octavia Warrenton*
E. E. Clive . . . . *Sir Humphrey Harcourt*

Jack-booted Michael Curtiz, who ordered on the empty horses and provided Niven with a title for a book, directed this super-hokum vehicle for Errol Flynn.

STORY

Soldier brothers Major Geoffrey and Captain Perry Vickers compete for the hand of Elsa, the colonel's daughter, while campaigning on the North West Frontier of India.

Surat Khan, a nasty thorn in the side of the British Raj, is intriguing with the Russians as part of his plan for ousting the British.

He organises the bloody massacre of Chukoti, and Geoffrey and Elsa only escape through the intervention of Surat Khan himself who owes the major a favour.

Later, the Khan openly joins the Russians and turns up, providentially, just before the famous charge. Geoffrey, who has been seething for a chance to avenge the massacre despite the Khan's gesture, countermands an order not to attack the enemy and leads the charge of the 17th Lancers.

He is mortally wounded by Surat Khan but kills him before dying, leaving Elsa in the arms of brother Perry.

NOTES

The Charge of the Light Brigade provided Niven with his first epic. Apart from his publicity, being heroically handled by Sam Goldwyn's praiserie, the Niven career was still mainly a thing of colourful rags and patches. As Captain Randall his main function was to decorate the mess, look dashing and die decently.

The film's eccentric story line was greeted with general derision although the popular papers, and certainly the public, delighted in the spectacle.

In the course of its production nasty accusations were made of ill-treatment of the horses, and three of them were certainly killed. Warners were prosecuted, convicted of cruelty and fined. The beneficial result of the case was that controls over Hollywood's use of animals were strengthened.

The emphasis on the North West Frontier, with scant regard for the historical realities, suggest an attempt by Warners to repeat the success Paramount had enjoyed the year before with Henry Hathaway's stunning *The Lives of a Bengal Lancer*.

'The acting is negligible, the bloodiness is all' said the *New Statesman* savagely.

The *Observer* noted sadly that the Union Jack was usually seen flying upside down but added 'The charge itself, once we get to it ...... is enormously effective.'

One of the campaigns of '36. Group of seasoned Hollywood fighting men (before and behind the camera) assembled for *The Charge of the Light Brigade* with Errol Flynn, of course, holding pride of place. David Niven, as a relatively raw recruit, in the back row on the far left.

BELOVED ENEMY

1937

Sam Goldwyn Inc. *Producer*: George Haight *for* Sam Goldwyn. *Director*: H. C. Potter. *Script*: John Balderston, Rose Franken, William Brown Meloney—*from a story by* John Balderston *with additional dialogue by* David Hertz. *Camera*: Gregg Toland. *Art*: Richard Day. *Music*: Alfred Newman. *Editor*: Sherman Todd. *Running time*: 90 minutes.

CAST

Merle Oberon . . . . *Helen Drummond*
Brian Aherne . . . . *Dennis Riordan*
Karen Morley . . . . *Cathleen*
Jerome Cowan . . . . *O'Rourke*
David Niven . . . . *Gerald Preston*
Henry Stephenson . . . . *Lord Athleigh*
Donald Crisp . . . . *Burke*
Ra Hould . . . . *Jerry*
Granville Bates . . . . *Ryan*

STORY

The setting is Dublin, the time the Irish 'troubles' of 1921. Revolutionaries fighting for Irish independence battle it out with British troops in the streets. Lord Athleigh, a top British civil servant, arrives to find a peace formula. He is accompanied by his daughter Helen and his secretary Gerald Preston.
Fate, and the fighting, throw Helen and Dennis Riordan, the Irish insurgent leader, into each other's arms.

But when Helen realises his true identity duty triumphs over love and she betrays him.
A trap is set but Riordan escapes. A remorseful Helen begs forgiveness and they part, vowing to come together when peace returns.
Helen works hard behind the scenes to effect that peace. It comes with Riordan signing a treaty with the British. Denounced by some of his compatriots as a traitor he is assassinated by a fanatic and dies in Helen's arms.

NOTES

The shadow of John Ford's *The Informer* hangs over this picture but once one has swallowed the little twists Hollywood usually gave to history, in this instance Merle Oberon solving the Irish troubles behind the backs of the historians, it turns out to be an effective thriller with a believable setting. David Niven, though still out of the main running, had an opportunity to put over more of the genuine Niven personality than usual and took it.
'David Niven . . . scores in the smaller role of Lord Athleigh's secretary; he has some humorous lines of which he makes the most', observed *Picturegoer*.
And *The Times* said: 'The English are treated with mild satire, sharpened by Mr. Henry Stephenson and Mr. David Niven.'
From the *New York Times* came the comment: 'It demanded the most convincing performances, and it received them from . . . David Niven . . .'

A word from the sponsor. Sam Goldwyn drops in on Merle Oberon and protégé Niven on the set of *Beloved Enemy*.

Niven brought a welcome touch of lightness to an effective but melodramatic tale of the Irish 'troubles'.

WE HAVE OUR MOMENTS

1937

Universal. *Associate Producer*: Edmund Grainger. *Director*: Alfred L. Werker. *Script*: Bruce Manning, Charles Grayson *from an original story by* Charles F. Belden and Frederick Stephani. *Camera*: Milton Krasner. *Art*: Jack Otterson. *Editor*: Frank Gross. *Running time*: 65 minutes.

CAST

Sally Eilers . . . . *Mary Smith*
James Dunn . . . . *John Wade*
Mischa Auer . . . . *Captain Enrico Mussetti*
Thurston Hall . . . . *Frank Rutherford*
David Niven . . . . *Joe Gilling*
Warren Hymer . . . . *'Smacksey'*
Marjorie Gateson . . . . . *Mrs. Rutherford*
Grady Sutton . . . . *Clem Porter*
Joyce Compton . . . . . . *Carrie*

STORY

Mary Smith, an attractive small-town school teacher, is destined to marry a dull local citizen, but determined to enjoy one last swing before declining into aspic she sets off on a pleasure trip to Europe.

On the ship she gets to know a charming society couple, Mr. and Mrs. Frank Rutherford, their bruiser bodyguard, 'Smacksey', and their friend, smoothie Englishman, Joe Gilling. They are, in fact, four crooks pretending to be top people, robbing anyone in sight and not above robbing each other.

They plant their loot on Mary at a moment when arrest seems imminent as detective John Wade appears on the scene. He falls for Mary but the course of true love falls foul of a series of complications during which Wade suspects Mary of being a crook and she suspects him. Matters are not helped as the party reach Monte Carlo by the arrival of Enrico Mussetti, the local chief of police. Wade ensures that matters are brought to a satisfactory and romantic conclusion.

NOTES

This little frolic—worth no more than the position of losing partner on a double bill—was something of a come-down after *Beloved Enemy,* but this one step forward followed by one step back has been the pattern of Niven's entire career, the combined fault of film men reluctant to risk good material on him and his own readiness to accept indifferent pictures without putting up enough of a fight.

Kine Weekly summed this one up: 'Preposterous but entertaining story' and observed: 'Thurston Hall, David Niven and Warren Hymer mix effectively as the crooks.'

Gus McCarthy, of the *Motion Picture Herald,* attended its sneak preview in a Los Angeles cinema and reported 'The well filled house demonstrated its enjoyment'. In those days of high jinks and hyperbole such a muted response almost amounted to a raspberry.

A nasty situation brewing with James Dunn. . . .

The situation gets even nastier.

This sort of scene, although it looks better in the picture, is the kind of thing that could happen to any up-and-coming actor in Hollywood in the 30s.

We Have Our Moments was the type of film Hollywood was turning out at a dime a dozen but it's interesting for an early sight of Niven as the crook with the heart of corn.

THE PRISONER OF ZENDA

1937

Selznick International. *Producer*: David O. Selznick. *Assistant to producer*: William H. Wright. *Directors*: John Cromwell, W. S. Van Dyke. *Script*: John Balderston, Wells Root, Ronald Ogdon Stewart—*from the novel by* Anthony Hope. *Art*: Lyle Wheller. *Music*: Alfred Newman. *Costume*: Ernest Dryden. *Interior Decoration*: Casey Roberts. *Camera*: James Wong Howe. *Special effects*: Jack Cosgrave. *Editors*: Hal C. Kern, James E. Newcom. *Running time*: 101 minutes

CAST

Ronald Colman	*Rudolph Rassendyll*
	King Rudolph V
Madeleine Carroll	*Princess Flavia*
Douglas Fairbanks Jnr.	*Rupert of Hentzau*
Mary Astor	*Antoinette de Mauban*
C. Aubrey Smith	*Colonel Zapt*
Raymond Massey	*Black Michael*
David Niven	*Captain Fritz van Tarlenheim*
Eleanor Wesselhoeft	*Cook*
Byron Foulger	*Johann*
Montague Love	*Detchard*
William Von Brincken	*Kraftstein*
Philip Sleeman	*Lanengram*
Ralph Faulkner	*Bersonin*
Alexande D'Arcy	*De Gauiet*
Torben Meyer	*Michael's butler*

STORY

Rudolph Rassendyll is the English distant cousin of the raffish King Rudolph of Ruritania. They meet by chance and that same night Rudolph, on one of his drinking sessions, is drugged by orders of the scheming Black Michael. Rudolph is due to be crowned the following day and if he does not appear for the ceremony loses the throne.

Rassendyll is persuaded to impersonate the king, a job which he reluctantly undertakes but admirably carries off. Few know of his impersonation. In the dark is Princess Flavia, the real king's betrothed. She finds the fake king a distinct improvement on the original version and he falls instantly in love with her.

The conspirators, temporarily foiled, strike again. The wicked Rupert of Hentzau kidnaps the drugged king and imprisons him in the virtually impregnable Castle of Hentzau. Rassendyll swims the castle moat, defeats Rupert in a fearsome sword fight and rescues the king. It then falls upon him to explain the true situation to the astounded Flavia and makes a sad but discreet exit for England. Flavia is left to take up her dutiful role at the side of the true king but a man no longer her true love.

NOTES

As Captain Fritz van Tarlenheim David Niven has a name rather more impressive than his part, and on the credits he just makes it over the cook. But

Niven very much in the background in this film.

Ronald Colman (seen with C. Aubrey Smith) dominated the picture but Niven's part was a perfect cameo.

With C. Aubrey Smith.

there are compensations. He offers a small, but perfect, contribution to a picture where all the elements—or almost all—combine to produce the best of many screen versions of Anthony Hope's effective and exciting piece of hokum.

He gets some pretty unbeatable backing: John Cromwell, responsible for most of the directing, is at his spacious best; the witty John Ogden Stewart touch is fully evident in the script; James Wong Howe produced some superb photography; Alfred Newman provided stirring music and all the art departments surpassed themselves (Lyle Wheller went on to win an Oscar for *Gone With the Wind*).

In 1971 John Cutts was enthusing over the 34-year-old picture in *Films and Filming*.

He wrote: 'One of those rare movies which seem, by some magic trick, to become more fascinating and beguiling with every passing year.'

Picturegoer said at the time: 'Aubrey Smith comes right into his own as the faithful Captain Zapt and David Niven scores as the king's aide-de-camp.'

With Ronald Colman.

DINNER AT THE RITZ

1937

New World. *Producer*: Robert T. Kane. *Director*: Harold Schuster. *Script*: Roland Pertwee, Romney Brent. *Camera*: Philip Tannura. *Running time*: 78 minutes.

CAST

Annabella	*Ranie Racine*
David Niven	*Paul de Brack*
Paul Lukas	*Philip de Beaufort*
Romney Brent	*Jimmy Raine*
Francis L. Sullivan	*Brogard*
Stewart Rome	*Racine*
Frederick Leister	*Tarade*
William Dewhurst	*Devine*
Tyrell Davis	*Duval*
Vivienne Chatterton	*Marthe*
Ronald Shiner	*Sydney*
Nora Swinburne	*Lady Railton*
Raymond Huntley	*Gibout*
Ralph Truman	*Auctioneer*

Launching Annabella.

STORY

In the middle of a party at his house Racine, a Parisian banker, is shot dead. He had been concerned about a conspiracy that could ruin his bank. He had revealed that he had posted a letter containing the names of six men, known only to himself, whom he thinks may be the guilty ones.

The letter never arrives and his death is assumed to be suicide while under financial pressure. His daughter Ranie believes otherwise and resolves to solve the mystery and expose the swindlers.

She is aided by an American detective and meets Paul de Brack, a debonair man about town (but really a government investigator on the same track). Her sleuthing takes her into various adventures and into some assorted, fashionable backgrounds including a visit to the French Riviera, a houseboat on the Thames and, inevitably, to dinner at the Ritz where the dénouement takes place.

It is the resourceful Paul who eventually unmasks the leader of the gang and forces him to return his ill-gotten gains. The hunt being up, the honour of the Racine family satisfied and justice done, the way is clear for Ranie and Paul to pursue a romantic course.

NOTES

Niven came home for his first starring part in a first feature made at Denham Studios on a loan-out from Goldwyn to Fox. (New World was the company's British production subsidiary.) The film was primarily a vehicle for 20th Century's new star discovery from France, Annabella, with some suitably aristocratic and glamorous settings.

No one seemed to have bothered much about providing a convincing story or logical development, but as compensation (or as camouflage) there was plenty of incident and for Niven a chance to grab a reasonable share of the limelight.

The *New York Times* noted a truly British addiction to afternoon tea among the characters. 'There was actually one scene where we thought we detected a crumpet crumb on Mr. Niven's collar.'

Of the film itself they didn't think an awful lot. 'It moves with Old World decorum and occasional touches of gout. Yet it has its virtues, Annabella, David Niven and Romney Brent among them.'

BLUEBEARD'S EIGHTH WIFE

1938

Paramount. *Producer/Director*: Ernst Lubitsch. *Script*: Charles Brackett, Billy Wilder—*from a play by* Alfred Savoir. *Camera*: Leo Tover. *Editor*: William Shea. *Art directors*: Hans Dreier, Robert Usher. *Musical score*: Frederick Hollander, Werner R. Heymann. *Sound*: Harry D. Mills. *Running time*: 85 minutes.

CAST

Claudette Colbert . . . . . *Nicole de Loiselle*
Gary Cooper . . . . *Michael Brandon*
Edward Everett Horton . *The Marquis de Loiselle*
David Niven . . . . *Albert de Regnier*
Elizabeth Patterson . . . . *Aunt Hedwige*
Herman Bing . . . . *Monsieur Pepinard*
Warren Hymer . . . . . . *Kid Mulligan*
Franklin Pangborn . . . *Assistant Hotel Manager*
Armand Cortes . . . . . . *Assistant Hotel Manager*
Rolfe Sedan . . . . *Floorwalker*
Lawrence Grant . . . . . . *Professor Urganzeff*
Lionel Pape . . . . *Monsieur Potin*
Tyler Brooke . . . . *Clerk*
Tom Ricketts . . . . . . *Uncle Andre*
Barlow Borland . . . . . *Uncle Fernandel*
Charles Halton . . . . . . *Monsieur de la Coste*

STORY

American multi-millionaire Michael Brandon—with seven unsuccessful marriages as well as a multitude of successful business deals behind him—is on the French Riviera and seeking to buy a pair of pyjamas. This produces an unlikely meeting with Nicole de Loiselle, the daughter of an impecunious French aristocrat. The result: he is in love again.

Nicole, unimpressed by his wealth, rebuffs him. This scandalises her father, the Marquis, who sees a chance of reviving the family fortune. Brandon, for whom rejection is a novel experience, is only fired to greater ardour.

He tries to buy his way into her favour, with disastrous results. Finally, succumbing to her father's entreaties, she agrees to marry Brandon, but makes it clear it's just his money she is after.

During their European honeymoon tour Nicole, fearing she will end as just another of his cast-off wives, tries a number of tricks to break his spirit, including the production of a charming but vapid escort in Albert de Regnier.

Her plans work only too well and Brandon decides she's too hot to handle and offers her a divorce. The well-heeled boot is now on the other foot and Nicole is in pursuit of Michael.

In the end, of course, Bluebeard is tamed.

NOTES

It was a brilliant stroke of Lubitsch to cast Gary Cooper as the much married millionaire instead of some conventionally sleek and urbane type. Cooper portrayed exactly the sort of man who might be marvellous with money but hopelessly *gauche* with the girls. David Niven as Albert may have been landed with yet another part as a foil, but his usual charm and his gift for portraying a sort of empty elegance where required supplied just the contrast the plot required.

Contemporary reviewers didn't take kindly to the casting of Gary Cooper in this sort of part and as far as they were concerned in this film Lubitsch lost his touch.

It seemed that millionaires were going through a bad patch in the socially conscious America of the period which probably accounts for this mysterious passage from the *New York Times*.

'In these days its bad enough to have to admire millionaires in any circumstances; but a millionaire with a harem complex simply can't help starting the bristles on the back of a sensitive neck.'

But the paper conceded that *Bluebeard's Eighth Wife* was '. . . enlivened by the supporting presence of Edward Everett Horton, Herman Bing, David Niven and Warren Hymer.'

This may be an opportune moment to point out that although the Niven memoirs *The Moon's A Balloon* provides entertaining reading they include some awful chronology.

The actor's reluctance to hang on to any of his reviews—which can provide useful records—may account for the fact he sometimes gets the sequence of his pictures in a muddle. In the case of *Bluebeard's Eighth Wife*, for instance, he records that he made it after completing *A Feather In Her Hat* and went

A comedy with Lubitsch, a sunny scene with Claudette Colbert came with *Bluebeard's Eighth Wife* but at this time Niven, in his big films, was still being overshadowed by bigger stars; in this case Gary Cooper.

on to his first starring role in *Thank You, Jeeves.* In fact, he made *A Feather In Her Hat* ten pictures and two years before *Bluebeard* and *Thank You, Jeeves* back in 1936.

This note is not added to rap Mr. Niven across the knuckles but to prevent perplexity and irritation spreading among his admirers in the face of apparent contradictions.

FOUR MEN AND A PRAYER

1938

20th-Century Fox. *Producer:* Kenneth MacGowan. *Director*: John Ford. *Script*: Richard Sherman, Sonya Levien, Walter Ferris *from the book by* David Garth. *Camera*: Ernst Sternad. *Editor*: Louis Loeffler. *Running time*: 85 minutes.

CAST

Loretta Young	*Lynn*
Richard Greene	*Geoff*
George Sanders	*Wyatt*
David Niven	*Chris*
C. Aubrey Smith	*Leigh*
J. Edward Bromberg	*Torres*
William Henry	*Rod*
John Carradine	*General Sebastian*
Alan Hale	*Furnoy*
Reginald Denny	*Loveland*
Berton Churchill	*Cherrington*
Barry Fitzgerald	*Mulcahay*
Claude King	*General Bryce*
Cecil Cunningham	*Piper*
Frank Dawson	*Mullins*
John Sutton	*Drake*

STORY

Colonel Leigh, a British officer serving in the Indian Army, is accused of causing the death of some of his troops, court-martialled and cashiered. On his return to England he is met by a gathering of his four sons, who refuse to believe him guilty.

The sons, Wyatt, a young barrister, Chris, an R.A.F. officer, Geoffrey, a diplomat and Rod, an Oxford undergraduate, band together to clear his name.

They suspect that an international munitions ring could be responsible. Then the colonel is murdered and robbed of vital documents.

The brothers continue their relentless detective work and a trail of clues lead them to India, South America and Egypt.

All, as far as the four are concerned, are under suspicion including Lynn, the attractive American girl in love with Geoffrey; one could say particularly Lynn, as her father is president of the munitions ring.

Eventually the real culprit is unmasked and the colonel's honour restored.

Four for vengeance. Richard Greene, George Sanders and William Henry join David Niven for the John Ford vendetta.

Four men and . . . Loretta Young.

Confrontation with Reginald Denny.

Tenderness with Loretta Young.

FOUR MEN AND A PRAYER

WITH **LORETTA YOUNG**

RICHARD **GREENE** AND GEORGE **SANDERS** DAVID **NIVEN** C. AUBREY **SMITH**

J. EDWARD **BROMBERG** WILLIAM **HENRY** JOHN **CARRADINE** ALAN **HALE** REGINALD **DENNY**

DIRECTED BY
JOHN FORD
ASSOCIATE PRODUCER
KENNETH MACGOWAN
SCREEN PLAY BY
RICHARD SHERMAN,
SONYA LEVIEN AND
WALTER FERRIS
FROM A BOOK BY
DAVID GARTH

A 20TH CENTURY-FOX PICTURE
DARRYL F. ZANUCK
IN CHARGE OF PRODUCTION

NOTES

As one examines the Niven career around this time it becomes increasingly clear that it was his less publicised quality of adaptability that was standing him in the best stead. He could turn from his true forte as a brilliant light comedian, decorating even the most vulgar comedy they might throw at him, to handling the straight dramatic role in a way that ensured he emerged with dignity even from the dingiest melodrama. There were a few occasions—very few—when his flair for ensuring his own survival deserted him; his Bonnie Prince Charlie comes unhappily to mind, as well as the unfortunate incident of *The Statue*.

In view of the reluctance of film men to give him the choicest parts and limited by the strangling contract system from hewing out his own path he seems to have managed his career with considerable adroitness.

If he had to work with the worst, he also worked with the best. This film may have been minor Ford but even minor Ford stands taller than most other films.

With Richard Greene and Alan Hale.

'It has been energetically told, compactly presented,' said the *New York Times*. 'In retrospect we discern a flaw or two in the plot skein ... but these reflections only occur after the fact; the camouflage is admirable...'

'The players are uniformly in excellent fettle. Miss Young has found a handsome new leading man in Richard Greene and good company in George Sanders, David Niven and William Henry.'

51

THREE BLIND MICE

1938

20th-Century Fox. *Producer*: Raymond Griffiths (billed as *associate producer*). *Director*: William A. Seiter. *Script*: Brown Holmes, Lynn Starling *from a play by* Stephen Powys. *Camera*: Ernest Palmer. *Editor*: James Morley. *Running time*: 75 minutes.

CAST

Loretta Young . . . . *Pamela Charters*
Joel McCrea . . . . *Van Smith*
David Niven . . . . *Steve Harrington*
Stuart Erwin . . . . *Mike Brophy*
Marjorie Weaver . . . . *Moira Charters*
Pauline Moore . . . . *Elizabeth Charters*
Binnie Barnes . . . . *Miriam*
Jane Darwell . . . . *Mrs. Kilian*
Leonid Kinskey . . . . *Young man*

STORY

It's the dawn of hope for Pam, Moira and Elizabeth—three sisters owning a tiny poultry farm—when they inherit 5,000 dollars. They decide to invest the money in a scheme to net one of them a rich husband and take all three of them out of the egg business.

Pamela is elected leader of the trio and she poses as an heiress with Moira (secretary) and Elizabeth (maid) forming her entourage. They begin operations at Santa Barbara, society's playground and knee deep in eligible rich.

They don't have to wait long for nibbles. Soon both Van Smith, a young aristocrat, and Steve Harrington, a wealthy playboy, are contending for Pam's hand. She falls for Steve but—shock of shocks—discovers he's a pauper. Sisterly obligations demand the suppression of emotion and a return to the hunt. Meanwhile Elizabeth, as befits her lowly station in the conspiracy, is rapidly succumbing to the appeal of Mike, the barman.

Love, naturally, must out in the end and Pamela is soon back with Van Smith, Moira is teamed with Steve and Elizabeth with her barman, who turns out to be the man with the money.

NOTES

As Loretta Young, by smuggling young Niven into her studio and giving him a chance to see the movie business in action, must be considered mainly responsible for inflaming his tentative ambitions to become an actor, it's appropriate that they should have made several pictures together.

After appearing with her in the Ford film *Four Men and A Prayer* this one seems very minor league. But nevertheless the *New York Times* noted it 'a facile and engaging romantic comedy' and remarked 'the principal quintet does quite nicely' while reserving their warmest praise for Binnie Barnes.

Three Blind Mice and David Niven waiting to pounce.

Three Blind Mice belongs to the era of Hollywood comedy when you could hear the crackle of bank-notes between every laugh. Joel McCrea and Loretta Young join Niven in typical stills' studio pose.

Loretta Young and Joel McCrea.

THE DAWN PATROL

1938

Warner Brothers. *Executive Producer*: Hal B. Wallis. *Associate Producer*: Robert Lloyd. *Director:* Edmund Golding. *Script*: Seton I. Miller, Dan Totheroh—*from an original story* Flight Commander *by* John Mark Saunders and Howard Hawkes. *Camera*: Tony Gaudio. *Art*: John Hughes. *Music*: Max Steiner. *Editor*: Ralph Dawson. *Running time*: 107 minutes

CAST

Errol Flynn . . . . *Captain Courtney*
David Niven . . . . *Lt. Scott*
Basil Rathbone . . . . *Major Brand*
Donald Crisp . . . . *Phipps*
Melville Cooper . . . . *Sergeant Watkins*
Barry Fitzgerald . . . . *Bott*
Carl Esmond . . . . *Von Meuller*
Peter Willes . . . . *Hollister*
Morton Lowry . . . . *Ronnie*
Michael Brooke . . . . *Squires*

STORY

In a corner of wartime France in 1915 a group of airmen of the Royal Flying Corps, few in number and with inadequate machines, confront the superior forces of the German air ace, von Richter.

Major Brand, the squadron's commander, has the daily nightmare of deciding who shall fly the necessary missions against the enemy with the certainty of a desperately high casualty rate.

Courtney, leader of 'A' flight, is the flamboyant, devil-may-care man of the squad, backed up by his friend, Scott, a lighter-hearted version of his idol and with a gentlemanly affection for the bottle.

Early in the action Scott, while aiding a fellow officer in trouble, is shot down. While Courtney is mourning his lost friend, Scott, as irrepressible as ever, turns up with an armful of champagne bottles. He managed to land his plane and make it back to base.

The Germans, eager to lure the British airmen out to combat, drop a pair of trench boots, more suitable than flying boots for land-locked airmen. Major Brand warns his men not to be stung into any ill-judged retaliation. But Courtney and Scott take off for a daring dawn raid on von Richter's base, blast it and return the boots. Courtney is downed but rescued by Scott.

The harassed Major Brand threatens Courtney with a court martial but he is suddenly recalled: it is Courtney, ironically, who replaces him.

It is now Courtney's ordeal to decide the fate of his fellow flyers. Before long he quarrels bitterly with Scott when he decrees that Scott's inexperienced young brother Ronnie should go into action; he is inevitably shot down.

An order arrives for a vital attack on a munitions dump; its success can stop a German advance. Scott volunteers for what is in fact a suicide mission. He and Courtney are reconciled over celebratory drinks but the latter ensures that Scott drinks too much. When the hour for take-off arrives Scott is still asleep and by this ruse Courtney is able to take his friend's place. His attack is spectacularly successful but he dies to achieve it.

It is left to Scott to shoulder the glories—and agonies—of command.

The stern face of duty. With Donald Crisp.

NOTES

This turned out to be a highly successful essay in the best Hollywood stiff upper lip manner of the adventures of the first of 'the few' before the R.A.F. existed. The cast was almost entirely British, director Edmund Golding handled the tear-jerking dramatics with restraint and the special effects were spectacular.

The Niven gift for providing light moments in heavy drama is well illustrated in *The Dawn Patrol* as he plays Errol Flynn's tippling fellow flying officer; irrepressible on the ground, unbeatable in the air.

David Niven brought into play one of his regular roles of the period; the man of action and daring but capable of the sort of flippant asides that lightened the conventional heavy heroics. He undertook the character played in an earlier film version of the story—made in 1930—by his close Hollywood friend, Douglas Fairbanks Jnr.

Niven now had a part full of dramatic meat as well as light relief. His success was noted appreciatively by the critics.

'Acting honours are fairly evenly divided,' said *Picturegoer*'s man. 'But I would give pride of place to David Niven as a pilot who quarrels with his best friend because, as a squadron commander, he has to order his inexperienced younger brother into the air on a raid which means almost certain death. It is a finely balanced, sincere performance.'

Film Weekly observed: 'Errol Flynn has never done a better job than his portrait of the carefree, young lieutenant ... David Niven is equally good as his happy-go-lucky friend. His clever changes of mood, from wild gaiety to agonised worry ... prove him to be a deeply sensitive, natural actor.'

The heroes with Basil Rathbone.

WUTHERING HEIGHTS

1939

A Samuel Goldwyn Production. *Producer*: Sam Goldwyn. *Director*: William Wyler. *Script*: Ben Hecht, Charles MacArthur—*from the classic novel by* Emily Brontë. *Camera*: Gregg Toland. *Art*: James Basevi. *Sets*: Julia Heron. *Music*: Alfred Newman. *Costumes*: Omar Kiam. *Editor*: Daniel Mandell. *Sound*: Paul Neal. *Special character make-up*: Blagoe Stephanoff. *Running time*: 104 minutes.

CAST

Merle Oberon . . . . *Cathy*
Laurence Olivier . . . . *Heathcliff*
David Niven . . . . *Edgar*
Flora Robson . . . . *Ellen Dean*
Donald Crisp . . . . *Dr. Kenneth*
Hugh Williams . . . . *Hindley*
Geraldine Fitzgerald . . . . . . *Isabella*
Leo G. Carroll . . . . *Joseph*
Cecil Humphreys . . . . *Judge Linton*
Miles Mander . . . . *Lockwood*
Romaine Callender . . . . *Robert*
Cecil Kellaway . . . . *Earnshaw*
Rex Downing . . . . *the child Heathcliff*
Sarita Wooten . . . . *the child Cathy*
Douglas Scott . . . . *the child Hindley*

STORY

Lockwood, new tenant of The Grange on the moors near the sinister old house Wuthering Heights, decides to call upon his neighbours. It is hardly the happiest of experiences. He is nearly overwhelmed by a fierce snow-storm and upon arrival finds the gloomy denizens of Wuthering Heights unwelcoming hosts.

Heathcliff, the master of the house, reluctantly allows him a room for the night when it is clear the storm makes his return impossible. In the night Lockwood is terrified by the sound of ghostly cries from outside the house. At the window he feels an icy hand upon his. On recounting his experience to the household, Heathcliff, with a wild cry, runs from the house.

It falls to Ellen Dean, Lockwood's housekeeper who knows all the secrets of Wuthering Heights, to tell Lockwood its grim story.

Edgar Linton marries Cathy in William Wyler's superb version of *Wuthering Heights*.

I am torn with *Desire*---tortured by hate!

SAMUEL GOLDWYN
presents

WUTHERING HEIGHTS

co-starring

MERLE OBERON · LAURENCE OLIVIER · DAVID NIVEN

with FLORA ROBSON · DONALD CRISP · GERALDINE FITZGERALD · *Released thru* UNITED ARTISTS

Directed by WILLIAM WYLER

Its owner, Earnshaw, father of a son and daughter and a man of philanthropic disposition, returns from a visit to Liverpool with a wild gypsy boy he found abandoned. He adopts him calling him Heathcliff after a dead son. His daughter Cathy becomes increasingly entranced with the rude but compelling boy, but his son Hindley takes a jealous dislike to him.

On the death of Earnshaw, and the passing of the power at Wuthering Heights to Hindley, life for Heathcliff becomes almost intolerable.

While out roaming the moor, Cathy and Heathcliff peep through the window of another neighbouring house, the home of the Lintons, where a ball is in progress. Dogs surprise them and Cathy is taken in but Heathcliff is contemptuously sent away.

Cathy is fascinated by the smooth and gracious life at the Linton home, and the suave and polished person of young Edgar Linton.

Heathcliff, who has tolerated life at Wuthering Heights only to be near Cathy, believes she now loves Edgar and rides away. Cathy tries to follow him but is thrown by her horse. Edgar finds her. In time, with Heathcliff vanished, Cathy and Edgar marry. Two years later a much changed but still morose Heathcliff returns. He has made his fortune in South America. He takes over Wuthering Heights by cornering the debts and obligations of Hindley, who has squandered the estate on the bottle.

Then begins Heathcliff's implacable revenge. Hindley is now the beggar at the table and Heathcliff marries

Laurence Olivier with Merle Oberon.

Edgar's sister Isabella and condemns her to a loveless life. On news that Cathy is dying however, Heathcliff rushes to her side, depriving Edgar of even a dignified place by the deathbed. She confesses it has been only him she has loved. He calls upon Cathy to haunt him. At the end of Ellen's story Lockwood learns that Heathcliff has been found dead on the moors; the two troubled spirits have been re-united at last.

NOTES

Considering that Emily Brontë's novel would be inevitably butchered to scale the story down to the time and scope available for a Hollywood costume epic of the period, Ben Hecht and Charles MacArthur produced a literate and highly effective script. William Wyler directed with distinction, the playing throughout was impressive and the photography won Gregg Toland an Oscar. Graham Greene, writing in the *Spectator,* was one of a few who took a cheerless view, rather perversely observing; 'A lot of reverence has gone into a picture that should have been as coarse as a sewer.' He thought it would have been better done in the spirit of an obscure French film of passion he remembered in which the lovers remained claustrophobically locked together in bed throughout without even the benefit of a change of linen. The proposition would probably have shocked Emily Brontë even more than it would have horrified the Hayes office.

For Niven this was his most prestigious picture since *Dodsworth* but he did everything, including risking a suspension, to avoid appearing in it.

He considered the part of Edgar unactable. Certainly, taken from the printed page, Edgar has an impossible role to play; even his charm and decency seem mere added evidence of his ineffectuality.

But Niven had scored frequently in his lighter roles at making the hapless man appealing and with increasing technical proficiency he was able to muster this weapon from his acting armoury to good effect, even in a drama of thunderous emotions; as a result, his Edgar Linton remains a living and touching portrait.

The *New York Times* sums up this aspect of the picture most significantly.

'The Lintons, so pallid, so namby-pamby in the novel, have been more charitably reflected in the picture. David Niven's Edgar, Geraldine Fitzgerald's Isabella are dignified and poignant characterisations of young people whose tragedy was not in being weak themselves but in being weaker than the abnormal pair whose destinies involved their destruction.'

The picture has its detractors today but *Movies on TV* in 1968 said: 'Emily Brontë's hypnotic, romantic novel is tastefully brought to the screen with the perfect cast' and gave it the top four star rating.

The overwhelming passion in *Wuthering Heights* belonged to Olivier's Heathcliff but David Niven was not snuffed out. Never before had his resourcefulness as an actor been better demonstrated than in his characterisation of Linton.

BACHELOR MOTHER

1939

R.K.O. Radio. *Producer*: B. G. DeSylva. *Director*: Garson Kanin. *Script*: Norman Krasna—*from a story by* Felix Jackson. *Camera*: Robert de Grasse. *Editors*: Henry Berman, Robert Wiss. *Running time*: 82 minutes.

CAST

Ginger Rogers . . . . *Polly Parrish*
David Niven . . . . *David Merlin*
Charles Coburn . . . . *J. B. Merlin*
Frank Albertson . . . . *Freddie Miller*
E. E. Clive . . . . *The Butler*
Elbert Coplen Jnr. . . . . *Johnnie*
Ferike Boros . . . . *Mrs. Weiss*
Ernest Truex . . . . *Investigator*
Leonard Penn . . . . *Jerome Weiss*
Paul Stanton . . . . *Hargraves*
Gerald Oliver-Smith . . . . *Hennessy*

STORY

Polly Parrish is a temporary sales assistant for the pre-Christmas rush period at the toy department of the giant J. B. Merlin store, run by slightly choleric tycoon J. B. Merlin himself and his playboy son, David.

While returning from her lunch break Polly spots a baby, wrapped in a blanket, toppling off the steps of an orphanage and rushes up and catches it in the nick of time . . . and just as the main door opens.

Toying with Ginger Rogers.

Assuming that Polly is delivering the baby to the home she is ushered in and grilled by the matron and doctor who discover her home address and place of work before taking the baby in under the impression she is the mother.

An investigator for the institution calls at the store to talk to Polly's boss. J. B. Merlin has left but David listens to the investigator's story. Full of good-hearted zeal he summons Polly and tells her that she has a permanent job and a rise in salary and says that he has a Christmas present for her as well. It turns out to be the return of her baby to her home. Polly is now beginning to despair of ever persuading anybody that she is not the baby's mother and had never seen it before.

Freddie, a colleague at the store, arrives to escort her to a dance contest. They solve the problem of what to do with the baby by taking it around and dumping it on the Merlin household.

David arrives as she leaves and chases after her to the dance hall but is thrown out. He decides to wait for her at her home.

David will not be convinced she is not the baby's mother so she bows to the inevitable and accepts the child.

Having started out on a philanthropic mission David finds himself drawn to Polly, much to the annoyance of the jealous Freddie.

The last straw for Freddie is when David takes Polly to a fashionable New Year party—dressed to the hilt in the best clothes he can find for her in the store.

Freddie sends the elder Merlin an anonymous note implying that David is the father of Polly's child. J. B., a softie at heart and crustily gratified at the prospect of a grandchild, demands David and Polly get married at once and make an honest grandfather of him.

After various maladroit machinations to persuade J. B. that he is wrong and thus avoid the need to marry, David discovers, naturally, that he really wants to marry Polly after all, and he doesn't mind the baby a bit. Polly decides to take the man and keep her own counsel.

Bachelor Mother provided David Niven with the ideal showcase to parade all his skills as a light comedian and, of course, gushes of his famous charm.

NOTES

This picture packaged for Niven all the elements he could handle so well; the character David Merlin was debonair but democratic, charming but ever so slightly dissolute, upper class but with the common touch, giddy but every inch the sterling prospective father and family man. He might have devised the part himself. Needless to say he did it every justice.

The genuine wit of Krasna's screenplay and the feather touch of director Garson Kanin made it one of the funniest and—most vital in the black closing month of 1939—one of the warmest films of the year. On the 1st September, just 18 days before the outbreak of World War II, it received critical and public acclaim.

61

The *Observer* said: 'I must insist that the most timely as well as the most engaging film of the week is a little thing called *Bachelor Mother*. Any picture that could hold one's undivided attention for 82 minutes during these days, a film that could make one relax and laugh and forget everything except the moving figures on the screen is entitled to top place in a reviewer's notice and his ungrudging admiration...

'Half the charm, of course, lies in the casting of the two leading parts which Ginger Rogers and David Niven play with a kind of perplexed and altogether persuasive delicacy...

'As for Mr. Niven, he is growing, film by film, into one of the best romantic comedians in the cinema. He has that light touch, combined with a bewildering courtesy and a faintly dog-like look of sadness, that endears young actors to audiences. If Ronald Colman should ever contemplate retirement, which heaven postpone, Mr. Niven would seem to be his legitimate successor.'

The *News Chronicle* remarked: 'Niven is unbeatable at this type of romantic comedy.'

The *Daily Sketch* was even more enthusiastic: 'But good as Miss Rogers is, Mr. Niven is better. He races through the film with so much gaiety and sophistication, with so much charm and understanding, I'd advise you to keep your girl friend from going to see this picture.'

The *New York Times* said: 'The spectacle of Miss Rogers and David Niven struggling forlornly to prove their innocence of parenthood and winning no credence at all is made triply hilarious by the sobriety of their performance... That is the way farce should be handled, with just enough conviction to season its extravagances.'

Ginger and David ... a ray of sunshine amid gathering storms.

ETERNALLY YOURS

1939

Walter Wanger Productions. *Producer*: Walter Wanger. *Director*: Tay Garnett. *Script*: Gene Towne, Graham Baker *with additional dialogue by* John Meeham. *Camera*: Merritt Gerstad. *Art*: Alexander Solitzen. *Editor*: Dorothy Spence. *Music*: Werner Janssen. *Running time*: 99 minutes.

CAST

Loretta Young . . . . *Anita*
David Niven . . . . *Tony*
Hugh Herbert . . . . *Benton*
Billie Burke . . . . *Aunt Abby*
C. Aubrey Smith . . . . *Bishop Peabody*
Virginia Field . . . . *Lola De Vere*
Broderick Crawford . . . . *Don Barnes*
Raymond Walburn . . . . *Mr. Bingham*
Zasu Pitts . . . . *Mrs. Bingham*
Eve Arden . . . . *Gloria*
Ralph Graves . . . . *Morrissey*
Lionel Pape . . . . *Howard*
Dennie Moore . . . . *Waitress*

STORY

Anita is about to marry her boyfriend Don Barnes, sturdy, upstanding, an ideal mate, but deadly dull. Then she finds her imagination caught up as if by magic by a man altogether more romantic, The Great Arturo, hypnotist, dare-devil stunt man and master illusionist, Tony to his friends.

She attends a matinée he gives for women only and after the performance stays on for a personal prediction session. . . .

Some time has passed when we meet The Great Arturo again, at the London Palladium, being dressed in his costume, loaded with the tricks of his trade, by his valet Benton.

On the stage he tells the audience he has a new wonder to offer them. He will create the perfect woman, using only those few chemicals actually the basic ingredients of all females. He tosses the chemicals into a vast retort, naming them as Beauty, Virtue, Modesty and Vanity. There is a great flash and from the billowing smoke steps—Anita. They have been married for several months in private and on the stage are partners in public.

The Great Arturo remains the glamorous figure of the footlights, the idol of women and the prey of gossip columnists and the stage struck. Anita, on the other hand, is quietly planning a small-town, dream home back in Connecticut. She sends money to her grandfather, Bishop Hubert Peabody, to buy the plot of land. When she reveals her aspirations to Tony he signs a contract for a world tour.

She goes with him but decides their destinies aren't linked after all and the bright life is not for her. She drops him and speeds back home to the welcoming arms of Aunt Abby who speedily organises the official disposal of The Great Arturo and Anita's marriage to dear, dreary Don.

Back at the footlights Tony, now an unhappy magician, pining for Anita, throws up his career and retires—irony of ironies—to that dream home of Anita's to live broken in spirit and pocket.

Discovered by his agent and Lola, an old stage partner,

Loretta Young and David Niven making magic.

he is persuaded to return to the stage—and is immediately offered an important benefit night at a country home.

Anita and husband are guests at the house. It is not long before Tony finds Anita still loves him and the Bishop conveniently discovers that the marriage to Don had a technical weakness and could be easily dissolved.

They are reconciled as The Great Arturo performs his last—and nearly fatal—feat, a dive from an aeroplane into the sea.

Don gracefully bows out and Tony and Anita head away from the footlights towards that home in the wilds.

NOTES

It was left to Hugh Herbert, at his dithery best, to salvage laughs from this rather heavy-handed comedy, as the mighty magician's right-hand man with an urge to be an illusionist too. Niven deploys the charm that woos the women off stage and tickles the tearbuds when down on his luck but can't make much out of The Great Arturo in action.

The *New York Times* summed it up: '*Eternally Yours* is an amusing and irresponsible picture though, on the whole, more irresponsible than amusing.

'It's real novelty is Mr. Niven as a magician and Miss Young as the lady he first carelessly causes to disappear, and then pursues to the far corners of the earth.'

THE REAL GLORY

1939

A Samuel Goldwyn Production. *Producer*: Sam Goldwyn. *Director*: Henry Hathaway. *Script*: Jo Swerling, Robert R. Presnell—*from the novel by* Charles L. Clifford. *Camera*: Rudolph Mate. *Music*: Alfred Newman. *Editor*: Daniel Mandell. *Art*: James Basevi. *Costumes*: Jeanne Beakhurst. *Special Photographic Effects*: R. O. Binger, Paul Eagler. *Sound*: Jack Noyes. *Running time*: 96 minutes.

CAST

Gary Cooper . . . . *Dr. Bill Canavan*
Andrea Leeds . . . . *Linda Hartley*
David Niven . . . . *Lt. McCool*
Reginald Owen . . . . *Capt. Hartley*
Broderick Crawford . . . . *Lt. Larson*
Kay Johnson . . . . *Mabel Manning*
Charles Waldron . . . . *Padre Rafael*
Russell Hicks . . . . *Capt. Manning*
Roy Gordon . . . . *Colonel Hatch*
Benny Inocencio . . . . *Miguel*
Vladimir Sokoloff . . . . *Datu*
Rudy Robles . . . . *Lt. Yabo*
Henry Kolker . . . . *The General*
Tetsu Komai . . . . *Alipang*
Elvira Rios . . . . *Mrs. Yabo*

Last stand in the Philippines.

STORY

A handful of American officers, backed by Dr Canavan, are left to lead local forces against a terrorist uprising in the Philippines. The Moros, a savage tribe in the hills, send spectacular assassins into the garrison from time to time who never fail to reach their victims and hack them to death in full view of the population. This keeps the islanders in a state of panic, convinced of Moro invincibility. It is left to Dr Canavan to reveal the Moros as vulnerable beings.

The danger of the situation doesn't prevent two women—the wife of the commanding officer Captain Manning and the wife of the second-in-command Captain Hartley—joining the group.

Soon Captain Manning is hacked to death in front of his wife and Captain Hartley takes command. He is aided by Lt. Larson and Lt. McCool, a curly headed Irishmen from a family with a long and honourable military record.

The Moros dam the river which provides the fort with its water, and soon cholera breaks out. Hartley, accompanied by Canavan, takes the bulk of his forces on an expedition to blow up the dam. This is just what the cunning Moros wanted. They attack the fort in strength. Lt. McCool, left in charge, rallies the natives with the help of Linda and puts up an heroic and bloody resistance, holding them at bay long enough to enable the troops to get back in time to the rescue, but is killed at the moment of victory.

NOTES

The Real Glory delivers just what the title promises, a compilation of all the best ploys of the adventure film, vigorously and savagely directed by Henry Hathaway with the goodies very good and the baddies positively revolting and, at times, as sinister as anything out of Dracula.

David Niven was playing strictly second fiddle to Gary Cooper in this one, even though he was a soldier and Cooper a doctor, which didn't stop the latter taking a fully aggressive part in the action. However the big spectacular last sequence—the siege of the fort—gave David Niven his own big piece of the action, the undivided attention of the leading lady and a gorgeous death scene.

The film was accepted with delight by most people

In *The Real Glory* David Niven (seen, below, with Broderick Crawford and Gary Cooper) was the likeable young man whose last-sequence heroic death brought a touch of pathos to a good boys' paper-style adventure yarn.

on its own terms. 'David Niven dies pleasantly and quietly. No one will mind that the Moro chief looks like the Djinn in an Aladdin pantomime, or that there is strong atmosphere of improbability, the film is much too good. With Gary Cooper at his most attractive, David Niven and Andrea Leeds looking charming, the film is recommended to adolescents of all ages', said the *New Statesman*.

Said the *Spectator*: 'It is directed by Henry Hathaway, who made *Bengal Lancers,* and the star is Gary Cooper with David Niven and others sparkling in the background.'

RAFFLES

1939

A Samuel Goldwyn Production. *Producer*: Sam Goldwyn. *Directors*: Sam Wood and William Wyler. *Script*: John Van Druten, Sydney Howard—*based on* The Amateur Cracksman *by* E. W. Hornung. *Camera*: Gregg Toland. *Art*: James Basevi. *Music*: Victor Young. *Costumes*: Travis Banton. *Editor*: Sherman Todd. *Sound*: Frank Mayher. *Running time*: 72 minutes.

CAST

David Niven . . . . *Raffles*
Olivia de Havilland . . . . *Gwen*
Dame May Whitty . . . . *Lady Melrose*
Dudley Digges . . . . *Mackenzie*
Douglas Walton . . . . *Bunny*
Lionel Pape . . . . *Lord Melrose*
E. E. Clive . . . . *Barraclough*
Peter Godfrey . . . . *Crawshay*
Margaret Seddon . . . . *Maud Holden*
Gilbert Emery . . . . *Bingham*
Hilda Plowright . . . . *Wilson*
Vesey O' Davoren . . . . *The Butler*

STORY

Mackenzie of the Yard is baffled. A daring and mysterious jewel robber, calling himself The Amateur Cracksman, is outwitting him at every turn. As dashing as he is skilful, his latest coup has been to steal a famous painting from the British Museum only to send it to a down-and-out actress he admired in his youth so that she could collect the reward by returning it.

Clearly the man is no ordinary member of the criminal classes. In fact, he is none other than A. J. Raffles, a famous cricketer and the nation's most popular athlete.

But a woman is his undoing. He falls in love with Gwen, the sister of his old school friend Bunnie Manders, and a girl, it's clear, who would not be seen dead, let alone smooching, with a professional burglar. Raffles decides on reformation. But as a result of sending back some recent loot he gives Mackenzie his first clue.

The detective and Raffles become part of a cricketing houseparty at the home of Lord Melrose, whose lady owns the famous Melrose emerald necklace. Is The Amateur Cracksman after it? This is what worries Mackenzie.

The emeralds are nicked, but by a rather nasty type of plebeian crook. But Raffles, as it happens, was after them despite his intentions to go straight: it was the only way he could bale Bunny out of trouble, as his old friend had made off with £1,000 of regimental funds.

Gwen now realises that her fiancé is a thief but tries to warn him that Mackenzie is now hot on his trail. Raffles evades the policeman and takes time off from the chase for another rendezvous with Gwen. Bunny has now confessed to her his wrong doings and she knows that even if Raffles is a crook he is a nobler specimen than average. They part, assured of meeting again, as Mackenzie closes in.

NOTES

Raffles was a part Niven was dying to play, and it was tailor made for him. Goldwyn dangled the part before his eyes at a time when after one of their regular rows, his contract was coming up for renewal and Leyland, Niven's agent, was haggling for a new deal with the producer. After keeping Niven in agonised

On the playing fields of Hollywood. *Raffles* was David Niven's big chance but it nearly slipped through his fingers.

With Olivia de Havilland.

uncertainty for a time, the inscrutable Goldwyn came to terms over the contract, handed Niven the part and gave him a royal welcome back to the studio.

More's the pity that it didn't turn out the success it should have been. The *New York Times,* in passing sentence, was merciful.

'Mr. Niven makes the game worth playing and the film worth seeing. His Raffles is one of the nicest tributes to burglary we have seen in many a year.'

Movies on TV was unsparing. 'Weakly done...obtrusive comedy tones creeping in...'

Raffles was the climax to the Sam Goldwyn Niven-building plan to launch the actor into the top star class. More, similar vehicles, would have followed. But World War II intervened.

With Douglas Walton.

THE FIRST OF THE FEW

(U.S. title: SPITFIRE)

1942

British Aviation Pictures Ltd. *Producer/director*: Leslie Howard. *Script*: Anatole de Grunwald, Miles Malleson—*from an original story by* Henry C. James, Kay Strueby. *Camera*: George Perinal. *Art*: Paul Sheriff. *Editor*: Douglas Myers. *Music*: William Walton. *Sound*: Harry Miller. *Running time*: 118 minutes.

CAST

Leslie Howard . . . . *R. J. Mitchell*
David Niven . . . . *Geoffrey Crisp*
Rosamund John . . . . *Diana Mitchell*
Roland Culver . . . . *Commander Bride*
Anne Firth . . . . *Miss Harper*
David Horne . . . . *Mr. Higgins*
J. H. Roberts . . . . *Sir Robert McLean*
Derrick de Marney . . . . . . *Sq. Leader Jefferson*
Rosalyn Boulter . . . . *Mabel Lovesay*
Herbert Cameron . . . . *MacPherson*
Tonie Edgar Bruce . . . . . . *Lady Houston*
Gordon McLeod . . . . *Major Buchan*
George Skillan . . . . *Mr. Royce*

As Wing Commander Geoffrey Crisp.

STORY

As Spitfire pilots wait the order to scramble on an air station somewhere in England, September, 1940, it seems an appropriate time to consider the life story of R. J. Mitchell who invented the plane.

On hand to tell it is the station commander, Wing Commander Geoffrey Crisp, a flying veteran and once Mitchell's test pilot.

War skies yield to the less threatening blue of 1922 with seagulls the most dangerous things in flight as Mitchell and his young wife Diana picnic on a cliff top. As an aircraft designer he is fascinated by the flying power of the gull and dreams of inventing an airplane with the same smooth and graceful lines.

Crisp, an unemployed ex-R.A.F. officer, joins Mitchell as test pilot. The designer, while working on planes of conventional style, still dreams of creating a stream-lined monoplane with a performance that would startle his contemporaries.

Authority is unimpressed. In the meantime he competes in the big air events of the day, sometimes with success, sometimes with failure: but finally wins the coveted Schneider Cup in his Supermarine S6.

The Mitchells, together with Crisp, are holidaying in Germany, visiting the glider clubs, when Mitchell discovers these are just a cover for training pilots in combat flying in defiance of the Versailles Treaty.

Fearing the airpower and the aggressive instincts of the Germans Mitchell hurries home and begins a frantic race to perfect his super plane, fighting official idiocy on the one hand and struggling to make do with inadequate funds on the other.

He falls ill and a fatal illness is diagnosed—one year to live providing he takes complete rest. But he refuses to abandon his experiments and lives just long enough to see the prototype Spitfire appear. It is acclaimed and its production begins in earnest.

Crisp ends his story as the call to battle comes for the Spitfire pilots. They take to the sky in planes that swoop and speed with the grace of a gull.

NOTES

Having abandoned his Hollywood career to return to Britain to enlist on the outbreak of war, Niven found

As the one major fictional character in a true story it fell to David Niven to embody all the men who encouraged aircraft inventor R. J. Mitchell in his efforts to build up an efficient fighting air force in the face of official opposition.

himself released 'for special duty' to make this film after nearly three years away from the camera. It was backed by the R.A.F. and intended to inspire the nation at a time of crisis. Films, or anything else, made with such intentions rarely survive their hour. But *The First of the Few,* though a trifle stolid to modern eyes, was an excellent example of how British film makers, provided with realistic subjects, rose to the challenge. Film critics like everyone else are not immune to events, but their respectful reception of this film seems in retrospect to have been fully merited. This is how the *Sunday Times* described it. 'The film is full of action, Schneider Trophy races, test flying and flashes from the Battle of Britain with which, pointing its moral, it begins and ends. It has moments of pathos and many scenes of agreeable, flippant comedy, contributed for the most part by David Niven who, as the test pilot working with Mitchell, gives a performance instinct with confidence and gaiety: one of his best performances up to now.'

This last sentiment was eched by *The Scotsman*: 'David Niven's performance as the test pilot is one of the best he has done.'

The *Observer* considered the interesting point that in a gallery packed with real people Niven played the one main character who was entirely fictional.

'Oddly enough, since Mitchell was a real man and Crisp is merely a symposium of test pilots, an imaginary creation, it is Mitchell who seems the figment, Crisp the flesh-and-blood character. David Niven's flippant assurance is just right here. The real-life story is the more real for his imagined presence; he gives the rather abstracted film a body.'

David Niven exchanged his true-life uniform of a major in the British army for RAF blue to make *The First of the Few*.

THE WAY AHEAD

1944

Two Cities. *Producers*: John Sutro, Norman Walker. *Director*: Carol Reed. *Script*: Eric Ambler, Peter Ustinov—*from a story by* Eric Ambler. *Camera*: Guy Green. *Editor*: Fergus McDonell. *Music*: William Alwyn. *Running time*: 115 minutes.

CAST

David Niven	*Lt. Jim Perry*
Raymond Huntley	*Davenport*
Billy Hartnell	*Sgt. Fletcher*
Stanley Holloway	*Brewer*
James Donald	*Lloyd*
John Laurie	*Luke*
Leslie Dwyer	*Beck*
Hugh Burden	*Parsons*
Jimmy Hanley	*Stainer*
Renee Asherson	*Marjorie Gillingham*
Penelope Dudley Ward	*Mrs. Perry*
Reginald Tate	*Commanding Officer*
Leo Genn	*Company Commander*
Mary Jarrold	*Mrs. Gillingham*
A. E. Mathews	*Colonel Warmsley*
Peter Ustinov	*Rispoli*
Tessie O' Shea *as herself*	

STORY

Jim Perry, a young officer just returned from Dunkirk as Britain reels back to the wall in World War II, is landed with the job of training raw recruits for the long journey to victory.

His heart sinks as he surveys his material, ranging from a former stoker to a prissy big-store floor-walker, but as he is hardly long from civvy street himself, a former Territorial army man (the peace time, spare time, soldiers), he and his unit can be viewed as a typical segment of the wartime citizen's army; a group viewed with disdain by the regular soldiers at the training depot.

Perry, determined to succeed in producing formidable fighters from his mixed bag, puts them through the whole gamut of preliminary training; square bashing, battle course, arms training and the rest. Set against

Granite-faced . . . with his squad of rookies and (behind him) his sergeant, that martinet of the British cinema, William Hartnell.

this background of hard grind are the usual soldierly pursuits of griping, jesting and romancing accompanied by the gradual revelation of their private lives. Training ended, Perry and his men embark on a crowded troopship for North Africa. The object: to help cut off Rommel's retreat from El Alamein.

The raw troops meet their first taste of real war when the ship is torpedoed with the loss of half the men. A destroyer takes the survivors the rest of the way.

Perry and his men find themselves stationed in an Arab village in Tunisia. It is not long before the village is under attack from German mortar teams. The platoon reject with contempt a call to surrender and sally forth to defeat the enemy. Perry orders the advance, secure in the knowledge that he has transformed his 'shower' into seasoned soldiers.

NOTES
David Niven, now a real life Lt.-Colonel in the British Army, conceived the idea of this film himself and it was backed by the Army. The inspiration was a short training film made about the training of Army recruits. Carol Reed, working on a subject for mass consumption, divided his work into two parts. The first half was almost a documentary in which the highly unromantic training schedules were cunningly spiced with the clash of fictional characters, and the second part,

with the men in action, provided a finale along the lines of the patriotic war adventure in fashion at the time.

It was not a method that entirely appealed to the reviewer of the *Sunday Times*.

'Carol Reed and his scriptwriters ... have admirably captured the qualities of mingled suspicion, irony and readiness to get on with the job which characterises many recruits to the British Army. Yet I must admit that, in spite of the lively dialogue of the first half of the film, in spite of the excellent playing of David Niven, Stanley Holloway, Billy Hartnell, Raymond Huntley, Jimmy Hanley and the rest of the recruits, it was not until the second half and embarcations for overseas that *The Way Ahead* seemed to show its real quality.'

But the critic ended: '*The Way Ahead,* in fact, is to be admired and recommended for its direction, its writing and its playing.'

Picturegoer said: 'The dialogue is completely natural as is the humour and there is nothing forced or phoney in a single foot of a wholly enjoyable and inspiring picture.'

Bosley Crowther in the *New York Times* wrote: 'In one scene, wherein he [David Niven] dresses down the trainees ... he accomplishes a truly heart-disturbing soldier's monologue.'

The peace of leave in the British countryside with wife (Penelope Ward) and child before the battle.

A MATTER OF LIFE AND DEATH

(U.S. title: STAIRWAY TO HEAVEN)

1945

The Archers (J. Arthur Rank). *Producers/directors/ script writers*: Michael Powell, Emeric Pressburger. *Camera*: Jack Cardiff. *Design*: Alfred Junge. *Music*: Allan Gray. *Costumes*: Hein Hekroth. *Editor*: Reginald Mills. *Colour control*: Natalie Kalmus. *Running time*: 104 minutes. Sequences in Technicolor.

CAST

David Niven . . . . *Squadron Leader Peter Carter*
Roger Livesey . . . . *Dr. David Reeves*
Raymond Massey . . . . *Abraham Farlan*
Kim Hunter . . . . *June*
Marius Goring . . . . *Conductor 71*
Robert Coote . . . . *Bob*
Robert Atkins . . . . *Vicar*
Edwin Max . . . . *Dr. McEwen*
Abraham Soafaer . . . . . . *Judge*
Kathleen Byron . . . . *Angel*
Richard Attenborough . . . . *Pilot*
Bonar Colleano . . . . *Pilot*
Joan Maude . . . . *Recorder*

STORY

Bomber pilot Peter Carter, his plane aflame, his crew dead or baled out, his parachute shot to ribbons, exchanges romantic words over the inter-com with an unknown American service girl who picks up his calls.

As the crippled plane descends towards the sea he bids a sad farewell to the voice he has fallen in love with and drops out of the bomber to certain death.

Miraculously, it seems, his life is spared. He is washed up on the sands; equally miraculously, within accosting distance of June, the girl he courted over the air.

They greet each other rapturously but Carter, outwardly barely harmed, is actually suffering serious injuries and June's brain specialist friend, Dr Reeves, diagnoses this when he hears of the strange hallucinations Carter is suffering.

In a metallic, monochrome Heaven a terrible blunder has taken place. Carter, due to die, has mistakenly survived. A representative of the Heavenly host, a dandified Frenchman who lost his head in the French revolution, is dispatched to explain the error to Carter and request his immediate presence among the spirits.

With Marius Goring.

Carter protests. Because of the mistake he has met and fallen in love and demands the right to appeal for an extension of life to enjoy it.

It is decided that an appeal will be held in Heaven and Carter will appear before a judge, represented by any advocate he cares to choose from the gallery of the great of all time. He will be prosecuted by one Abraham Farlan, the first man to die in the American War of Independence and no friend of any Briton.

Carter picks Dr Reeves to represent him and the doctor is killed off to ensure his availability. As the trial begins in Heaven an operation on Carter begins on earth. As love conquers all in the other world and he is granted his extension so he comes successfully through his operation in the world below.

NOTES

The team of Powell and Pressburger represented a unique element in British films: they frequently chose lofty themes, cast them with distinguished actors, indulged in remarkable feats of cinematic bravura, were imaginative and innovatory, enjoyed enormous popular acclaim but were consistently totally damned, or damned with faint praise, by most of the critics. Their case seems to bear comparison with the composer Meyerbeer—although he was, at least, generally accorded to be a genius in his life-time—a man of great craftsmanship, fully exploiting the operatic medium, exploring new paths but whose works seemed too carefully contrived, too carefully designed for popular appeal and where the grand subjects too often emerged as merely trivial.

In the case of *A Matter of Life and Death* the matter turned out to be trite—the great cosmic debate was twaddle—but the manner was bold and imaginative. There might have been a few outraged minds but not a bored heart in the house.

As every Powell and Pressburger film became an occasion of some sort this was a useful bridge between the Army and the resumption of his acting career for Niven. It was a film that became even more controversial than usual. It was the choice for the first of the Royal Command Film Performances. It was considered a poor film for such an honour (and virtually every Royal Command Film has beeen criticized on similar grounds ever since). It was also deemed grossly slanted to the American market and (preserve us!) anti-British.

'There will be widespread editorial indignation at the choice for our first Royal Film Performance,' thundered the *Daily Graphic* in its leader, 'of a picture which might have been made specially to appeal to isolationist and anti-British sentiments in the United States.'

It did get some flattering notices in America. The *Journal-American* said: 'Beautifully written, beauti-

In the fantasy world of Powell and Pressburger with Roger Livesey and Kim Hunter.

fully acted, beautifully executed ... You would think such formidable merits would add up to quite a film—and darned if they don't.'

'An extraordinary film, clearly one of the three or four best of the year,' said the *New York Post*.

The British reviewers found at least some things to admire. 'Yet this film,' concluded *Tribune*'s notice 'whether you find its philosophy half-baked or not, is down-right good cinema, doing things that couldn't be done in any other medium.'

'The main trouble with *A Matter of Life and Death,* which is original in conception, honestly acted by Mr. Niven and Kim Hunter,' said the *Observer,* 'is that it leaves us in grave doubts whether it is intended to be serious or gay. When they tell me that it is a "stratospheric joke" I reply that a matter of life and death can never be a good joke.'

'David Niven's handsome, well-spoken young airman, Kim Hunter's pleasant, competent girl are the characters of journalism and the novelette.'—*Sunday Times*.

David Niven came out of the whole controversial operation (on and off screen) pretty well.

'David Niven, as the pilot, gives the thoughtful, whimsical joke a warm and human heart,' said the *Sunday Express*.

Said the *Daily Telegraph*: 'David Niven has done nothing quite so good as his airman trembling on the brink of a nervous breakdown without ever lapsing into hysteria.'

THE PERFECT MARRIAGE

1946

Paramount. *Producer*: Hal Wallis. *Director*: Lewis Allen. *Script*: Leonard Spigelgass—*from the play by* Samson Raphaelson. *Camera*: Russell Metty. *Music*: Frederick Hollander. *Costumes*: Edith Head. *Running time*: 88 minutes.

CAST

Loretta Young . . . . *Maggie Williams*
David Niven . . . . *Dale Williams*
Nona Griffith . . . . *Cookie Williams*
Eddie Albert . . . . *Gil Cummings*
Virginia Field . . . . *Gloria*
Jerome Cowan . . . . *Addison Manning*
Rita Johnson . . . . *Mabel Manning*
Nana Bryant . . . . *Mrs. Cornelia Williams*
Charles Ruggles . . . . *Dale Williams Snr.*
Luella Gear . . . . *Mrs. Dolly Haggerty*
Howard Freeman . . . . . *Peter Haggerty*
Zasu Pitts . . . . *Rosa*

THE STORY

Dale (an aeronautical engineer) and Maggie (editor of a fashion magazine) are celebrating their 10th wedding anniversary. They are, in the eyes of friends and relatives, an ideally happy couple.

Some of the friends drop in to join the celebration. Dale makes it known, quite clearly, they would sooner be alone. Maggie thinks he was rude and a row blows up. Dale is banished for the night to his study.

Friend Gloria, a divorcée, drops in and smells trouble. She pointedly emphasises the miseries of unmarried life. The Williams, shocked, agree they must stay together. But Dale's male chauvinist attitude to the situation outrages Maggie. She promptly begins divorce proceedings.

After a flurry of misunderstanding Dale is planning to marry Gloria and Maggie to marry an old boy-friend, Gil. But ten years of togetherness exerts a powerful pull and the pair come together again.

A typical publicity still from the studios designed, it seems, to present the stars in the silliest possible light. The ladies are Virginia Field and Loretta Young with Eddie Albert. The film, *The Perfect Marriage,* lived up to this spirit.

NOTES

After six years away at the war, Hollywood's welcome home present for David Niven was this tosh. The slight was not lost on reviewers who responded sympathetically.

'*The Perfect Marriage* is another film about disillusionment and reconciliation in a mansion with constant evening dress, played by Loretta Young, brightly, and David Niven, sheepishly, and no wonder.'—*Sunday Times*.

'The film, which has a few amusing lines and Miss Zasu Pitts, pretends at a sophistication never present even in the luxurious sets, and Mr. Niven, that most admirable and sophisticated actor, seems to think that if he can keep quiet enough the whole thing will turn out to be a delusion.'—*The Times*.

'My strong regard for David Niven prompts me to say very little about *The Perfect Marriage*.'—*Observer*.

It was nice to be making yet another film with old friend Loretta Young but the picture better justifies the Niven look below than the one above.

MAGNIFICENT DOLL

1946

Universal. *Producer*: Jack H. Skirball, Bruce Manning. *Director*: Frank Borzage. *Script*: Irving Stone. *Camera*: Joseph Valentine. *Art*: Alexander Golitzen. *Editor*: Ted J. Kent. *Running time*: 90 minutes.

CAST

Ginger Rogers . . . . *Dolly Payne*
David Niven . . . . *Aaron Burr*
Burgess Meredith . . . . *James Madison*
Horace McNally . . . . *John Todd*
Frances Williams . . . . *Amy*
Robert H. Barrat . . . . *Mr. Payne*
Grandon Rhodes . . . . *Thomas Jefferson*
Henri Letondal . . . . *Count D'Arignon*
Joe Forte . . . . *Senator Ainsworth*
Erville Alderson . . . . *Darcy*

STORY

Delectable Dolly Payne is running a boarding house with her mother, having been left fatherless and a widow. It's the infancy of independent America and the state of the nation is far from stable.

Her beauty being something of a by-word the Payne's boarding house is a magnet for admiring young men, politicians among them. She is much fancied by the dashing and charming Senator Aaron Burr, a man scheming for power.

Another wooer is Congressman James Madison, a gentler and more honourable gentleman. Dolly cannot decide upon whom to bestow her affections but her mind is made up when Aaron Burr, tactlessly, reveals his ambitions to sieze power and become Emperor of the Americans.

Dolly marries Madison, who is President Jefferson's Secretary of State, and moves into the newly built White House.

Burr, meanwhile, has brought his schemes to fruition and has rallied a rabble army to his side. Overthrown and jailed, he is saved from a lynch mob by the interventional and lyrical oratory of Dolly. She argues that a live traitor is safer than the memory of a martyr. Burr slinks off to Europe and oblivion. Dolly is set for a glamorous career as the wife of the man due to become the 4th president of the U.S.A.

Niven the power-mad politician.

With Ginger Rogers and (below) Burgess Meredith.

NOTES

David Niven described the script of this one as 'gibberish' and the casting as idiotic but accepted the part to save another row with Goldwyn.

The story purported to be factual but its slice of American history—and such personalities as Dolly Madison and the traitor Aaron Burr—would not have meant much to the average British audience and so the distributor tried to pep it up by issuing the familiar modest slogans:

UNFORGETTABLE IN ITS SPECTACULAR MAGNIFICENCE ... THE STORY OF THE LUST FOR POWER OF AMERICA'S MOST INFAMOUS TRAITOR! SPECTACLE ... AS STARTLING AS THE RAGE OF MOB VIOLENCE!

To which the *Daily Mail* retorted: 'No duller case has ever been made out for liberty.'

'David Niven plays Aaron Burr as if he were cheering on the boat race,' pronounced the *Daily Express* with equal uncharity.

'Mr. Niven a very smooth villain,' said the *Graphic* more kindly and the *Sunday Times,* equally well intentioned, noted: 'David Niven as Aaron Burr looking traitorous in a gentlemanly sort of way.'

Time wrote wearily: 'Some day the moviemakers may discover they can make history wonderfully believable and exciting by just sticking roughly to the facts.'

Romance with Ginger in a film that was, to use one of the actor's favourite phrases, absolute gibberish.

Suave but rotten ... not a role to suit Niven.

THE OTHER LOVE

1947

Enterprise Productions: *Producer*: David Lewis. *Director*: André de Toth. *Script*: Ladislas Fodor and Harry Brown—*from a short story by* Erich Maria Remarque. *Camera*: Victor Milner. *Art*: Nathan Juran. *Music*: Miklos Rozsa. *Editor*: Walter Thompson. *Running time*: 97 minutes.

CAST

Barbara Stanwyck . . . . *Karen Duncan*
David Niven . . . . *Dr. Anthony Stanton*
Richard Conte . . . . *Paul Clermont*
Gilbert Roland . . . . *Croupier*
Joan Lorring . . . . *Celestine Miller*
Lenore Aubert . . . . *Yvonne*
Maria Palmer . . . . *Nurse Huberta*
Natalie Schafer . . . . *Dora Shelton*
Edward Ashley . . . . *Richard Shelton*
Richard Hale . . . . *Professor Linnaker*

STORY

Karen Duncan, a brilliant concert pianist, is admitted to the Mount Viergo Sanatorium in Switzerland, an institution very much in the private sector of medicine and run by dashing Dr. Anthony Stanton, a rich tonic for the women patients in his own right.

Karen is smitten, of course, and adds palpitations to her other ills. The doctor assures her that, although he likes to keep things friendly, in her own interests the régime will be demanding.

The death of a patient makes Karen suddenly lose faith in—but not entirely her love for—the doctor and she goes off for a wild whirl with racing driver Paul Clermont while she still has the strength.

In the end the devoted Dr. Stanton wins her back. They marry and the doctor tries to convince Karen she is well on the road to recovery.

But one evening she quietly dies while listening to the doctor trying to play one of her favourite piano pieces—although the two events are unconnected.

NOTES

This is the sort of role that requires a strong stomach as well as a good bedside manner and Niven manfully managed to bring both to the part but couldn't counter André de Toth's maudlin treatment and the heavily unsympathetic performance of Barbara Stanwyck.

The *New York Times* said: 'It abounds in the usual emotional suppositions and clichés familiar to drama assuming the inviolability of a woman's heart.'

Movies on TV gives it 2½ stars (fair plus) and says: 'Fair romantic drama. Good performances.'

With Barbara Stanwyck . . . but the outlook was bleak.

Lighter moment among some pretty purple passions.

Niven needed to polish up his bedside manner for this one as a doctor in charge of a Swiss sanitorium. Barbara Stanwyck is the concert pianist patient he falls for.

THE BISHOP'S WIFE

1947

A Samuel Goldwyn Production. *Producer*: Samuel Goldwyn. *Director*: Henry Koster. *Script*: Robert E. Sherwood, Leonardo Bercovici—*from the novel by* Robert Nathan. *Camera*: Gregg Toland. *Music*: Hugo Friedhofe. *Editor*: Monica Collingwood. *Art*: George Jenkins, Perry Ferguson. *Costumes*: Sharaff. *Running time*: 105 minutes.

CAST

Cary Grant . . . . *Dudley*
Loretta Young . . . . *Julia Brougham*
David Niven . . . . *Henry Brougham*
Monty Woolley . . . . *Professor Wutheridge*
James Gleason . . . . *Sylvester*
Gladys Cooper . . . . *Mrs. Hamilton*
Elsa Lanchester . . . . *Matilda*
Sara Haden . . . . *Mildred Cassaway*
Karolyn Grimes . . . . *Debby Brougham*

STORY

Henry Brougham, an Episcopalian bishop, is tending to lose touch with his flock, including his own nearest and dearest, wife Julia and daughter Debbie. The trouble is that he is too obsessed with grandiose plans for a new cathedral. To make matters worse he has to cope with the rich and overbearing zealot, Mrs. Hamilton.

When things are really getting him down, he does the natural thing. He prays to God for help. Help arrives, in the personable shape of a very worldly looking angel named Dudley.

Dudley brings joy to all, including the neglected bishop's wife and the vulnerable adolescent, Debbie. But Dudley never actually oversteps the mark. Julie begins to fall for him. Henry, realising it, orders him out of the house.

But, before he returns to the beyond, Dudley does a little more of good-will spreading, including transforming the character of Mrs. Hamilton.

Before midnight on Christmas Eve he returns to the bishop's house to say goodbye. He tells Henry not to worry about a thing. By the next day no one, including the family, will ever remember he had been there.

And that's how it turns out on Christmas morning with the bishop and wife reconciled and bristling with seasonal good cheer.

NOTES

Samuel Goldwyn, in a burst of true movie mogulism, played havoc with this production. After it had been shooting a fortnight he stormed in dissatisfied with the results and fired the original director, scrapped the script and pulled down the sets at a reputed cost of 800,000 dollars, and started again.

It meant a worrying time for the actors and not, perhaps, the most auspicious beginning to Niven's return to his old stable. The results, as far as the box-office were concerned, were sensational, which is more than can be said for the critical reception.

This was a bleak time for Niven, as his much beloved first wife Primmie had died tragically earlier in the year. It was not an easy task to face the disciplines of light comedy; the circumstances may account for the occasional touchingly lost air in his performance.

His tragedy didn't touch the hearts of the critics—perhaps it shouldn't have done, anyway—but surely

Cary Grant, Niven's great rival in the Hollywood light comedy field, joined him (in the part of an angel) as he played a bishop (with Loretta Young as the bishop's wife). The critics greeted the film with noticeable lack of piety.

Niven . . . 'touchingly lost air.'

Niven was to have played the angel, and Cary Grant the bishop. But Grant pleaded with Goldwyn for the more positive part of the angel. The roles were reversed.

a modicum of sympathy might have been expected. They murdered the picture.

'Not all the charm and intelligence of Cary Grant . . . can lighten the uninspired, saccharine mixture,' said *Reynolds News*.

'Mr. Niven's jaunty, moustached bishop and Cary Grant as an angel are equally unbelievable,' snorted the *Daily Herald*.

'It is the Protestant come-back to the deadly successful R.C. propaganda of *Going My Way* and *The Bells of St. Mary's*. *The Bishop's Wife* surpasses in tastelessness, equals in whimsy and in technique falls well below those crooning parables,' fumed the *News Chronicle*. 'It is really quite a monstrous film.'

'The picture is hardly a masterpiece but it has an attractive cast,' conceded *The Star*.

It was the *Sunday Pictorial* that provided the nearest thing to a rave review: 'It's all very polished and artificial but fair enough fun.'

The picture was chosen as the second Royal Command Performance which can only have irritated the critics more. *The Bishop's Wife* certainly went through hell, but it wears better than many films its critics treated with greater generosity.

BONNIE PRINCE CHARLIE

1948

With Margaret Leighton.

London Films and British Lion Production Assets. *Producer*: Edward Black. *Director*: Anthony Kimmins. *Script*: Clemence Dane. *Camera*: Robert Krasker. *Art*: Vincent Korda, Wilfred Shingleton, J. Bato. *Music*: Ian Whyte. *Costumes*: George K. Benda. *Editor*: Grace Garland. *Running time*: 118 minutes. Technicolor.

CAST

David Niven	*Prince Charles Stuart*
Margaret Leighton	*Flora Macdonald*
Judy Campbell	*Clementine Walkinshaw*
Jack Hawkins	*Lord George Murray*
Morland Graham	*Donald*
Finlay Currie	*Marquis of Tullibardine*
Elwyn Brook-Jones	*Duke of Cumberland*
John Laurie	*Blind Jamie*
Hector Ross	*Glenaladale*
Hugh Kelly	*Lt. Ingleby*
Charles Goldner	*Captain Ferguson*
Henry Oscar	*James III*
Martin Miller	*George II*
Franklin Dyall	*Macdonald*
Herbert Lomas	*Kinloch Moidart*
Ronald Adam	*Macleod*
John Longdon	*Colonel O' Sullivan*
James Hayter	*Kingsburgh*

STORY

It's a time of high hopes for the Jacobites with Charles Stuart, 'The Young Pretender', on his way home from Rome to lay claim to the English throne for the Stuart cause.

Bonnie Prince Charlie rallies the chiefs of the clans to his side upon landing in Scotland and begins a triumphal march to London, his campaign launched with a glittering victory at the battle of Prestonpans. But there is dissention in the Scottish camp, and the prince and his general, Lord George Murray, are in little accord when it comes to agreeing tactics. Eventually the fires kindled at Prestonpans are scattered in ashes at Culloden. The ill-equipped and inexperienced rebel armies are savagely crushed by the English troops and those who escape head back to the safety of their homes.

Charlie, with a few faithful followers, is hunted

Hour of disaster. This film inflicted upon Niven the biggest defeat of his career. The new, blond hair-style even aroused derision.

through the heather as he attempts to escape into exile. His cause is lost and his situation hopeless. But a simple Scots girl, Flora MacDonald, rows him to safety, disguised as a maidservant, across the sea to Skye.

NOTES

This is a milestone (or perhaps one should say a millstone) in Niven's career that can't be glossed over. It would be discreet to remark that it was, after all, a *success de scandale* if nothing else.

The actor certainly didn't want to make the picture but that was more for reasons of personal convenience than doubts about the enterprise. But soon after arriving from Hollywood he caught, as he wrote, the scent of disaster.

The picture, for Alexander Korda's London Films, took nearly a year to complete and cost nearly a million pounds, which was about double its initial budget, a vast sum in 1948, even by the standards of free-spending Korda.

Hardly a thing went right. 'I felt sorry for him (Korda) but I felt much sorrier for myself as the Bonnie Prince who would assuredly bear the blame for the impending debacle . . .' wrote Niven afterwards.

He was so right. 'David Niven looking as much at home among the Highlanders as a goldfish in a haggis,' said the *Sunday Graphic*.

'The picture is not lacking in moments of unconscious levity, what with David Niven, as Prince Charlie, rallying his hardy Highlanders to his standard in a voice barely large enough to summon a waiter,' wrote the *New Yorker*.

'Sad to say . . . David Niven disappoints . . . He is handsome enough but flaxen hair no more becomes him than it did Olivier's *Hamlet*'—*The Star*.

'Mr. David Niven has much of the fugitive charm that goes with the part, but the film refuses him the material he needs and only occasionally does his performance blaze up in flame and spirit—the heather is seldom alight and, when it is, the Technicolor fires are crude'—*The Times*.

David Niven's 'fugitive charm' that had stood him in good stead seemed to be eroding rapidly under the strain of deteriorating scripts and parts.

Bonnie Prince Charlie may not, as some have claimed, be the greatest single disaster in the history of British films; among a number of contenders it is difficult to apportion correctly the dishonours, but it was certainly high in the list.

Time has made it the film industry's biggest joke. But the joke turns a little sour when one reflects how extravagance, recklessness and sheer bungling administration during the fat and prosperous years left the British film industry so poor and vulnerable when the hard times came along.

ENCHANTMENT

1948

A Samuel Goldwyn Production. *Producer*: Samuel Goldwyn. *Director*: Irving Reis. *Script*: John Patrick —*from the novel by* Rumer Godden. *Camera*: Gregg Toland. *Art*: George Jenkins. *Music*: Emil Newman. *Editor*: Daniel Mandell. *Running time*: 99 minutes.

CAST

David Niven . . . . *General Sir Roland Dane*
Teresa Wright . . . . . . *Lark Ingoldsby*
Evelyn Keyes . . . . . . *Grizel Dane*
Farley Granger . . . . . . *Pilot Officer Pax Masterson*
Jayne Meadows . . . . . . *Selina Dane*
Leo G. Carroll . . . . . . *Proutie*
Philip Friend . . . . *Pelham Dane*
Shepperd Strudwick . . . *Marchese Del Laudi*
Henry Stephenson . . . . *General Fitzgerald*
Colin Keith-Johnston . . *The Eye*
Marjorie Rhodes . . . . . *Mrs. Sampson*

STORY

It's World War II but aged General Sir Roland Dane, in the dignified surroundings of his London home, is ruminating about the past, not his glories but his one big mistake.

Grizel Dane, an American serving in Britain driving an ambulance, makes a surprise visit. She is the grand-daughter of Roland's elder-brother Pelham.

Before you can say 'Take cover' Sir Roland is launching into the story of his life.

The three Dane children (Roland, Pelham and sister Selina) grew up with Lark, an orphan girl. The boys got along with her famously but not Selina. Roland falls in love with Lark and, in due time, now an Army officer, proposes marriage. Even though she has had a good offer from the young Marchese Del Laudi, Lark accepts with alacrity.

This doesn't suit the bitchy Selina who arranges, through high family connections, to have Roland

With Teresa Wright.

Buried under the make-up and about to reminis ... with Evelyn Keyes.

assigned to Afghanistan and convinces Lark that marriage would damage Roland's career.

Heart-broken, Lark makes the sacrifice and elopes to Italy with the handy Marchese. Roland, enraged, severs all relations with Selina. Now he is aged and alone.

There seems a moral in all this for Grizel. She's recently despatched in cavalier fashion a British pilot, Pax Masterson (by an extraordinary coincidence another distant relative of the general). The general warns her not to tamper with happiness, and to ponder upon his own fate. She takes the lesson to heart and returns to Pax.

NOTES

Pax Vobiscum is, perhaps, the best tail-piece for this plot. But it wasn't, as it happened, as bad as it sounds. Comment was kindly.

'Little addicted though I am to these four-in-hand romances I must give the film credit for sensitive direction and playing capable of extracting emotion from situations that have become the clichés of the screen,' said the *Sunday Times*.

The *Daily Mail* was quite warm, too. 'An elderly party looks back, a young party looks forward, and a patchwork of flashbacks shows what three generations of uncles, aunts and cousins were up to during the previous fifty years.

'They weren't, in this case, up to very much. But the little family anecdotes are played with a disarming sincerity and skill by Teresa Wright, David Niven and Evelyn Keyes with some welcome acid by Jayne Meadows.'

There was still, obviously, charm enough in the Niven *persona* to subdue criticism despite recent hard knocks.

Flashback melts the make-up and the years away.

With Farley Granger.

A KISS IN THE DARK

1949

Warner Brothers. *Producer*: Jack L. Warner. *Director*: Delmer Davies. *Script*: Harry Kurnitz—*from a story by* Everett and Devery Freeman. *Music*: Max Steiner. *Camera*: Robert Burks. *Art*: Stanley Fleischer. *Editor*: David Weisbart. *Running time*: 86 minutes.

CAST

David Niven . . . . *Eric Phillips*
Jane Wyman . . . . *Polly Haines*
Victor Moore . . . . *Horace Willoughby*
Wayne Morris . . . . *Bruce Arnold*
Broderick Crawford . . . . *Mr. Botts*
Joseph Buloff . . . . *Percy Danilo*
Maria Ouspenskaya . . . . *Mme. Karina*
Kurt Bois . . . . *Schloss*
Percival Vivian . . . . *Benton*
Raymond Greenleaf . . . . *Martin Soames*

STORY

Eric Phillips, a meek and mild concert pianist, is dominated by his manager, Percy Danilo. The pianist is visited by one Horace Willoughby, an obvious eccentric. He informs Eric that he is the new owner of a run-down apartment block, which Danilo has bought as an investment for him. That's the dubious good news. The bad news is that because repairs required by the building inspectors have not been carried out he is liable to arrest.

Eric visits his new property in a panic. It's peopled by odd characters, one of whom promptly punches him on the jaw. But a pretty model, Polly, tends his injuries. So he's twice smitten. The second time with love. But that brings him into head-on collision with brawny insurance salesman Bruce Arnold, Polly's fiancé.

As a concert pianist (with Maria Ouspenskaya and Jane Wyman) in a comedy that hardly ever struck the right note.

The course of true love is not made any smoother by Danilo who disapproves of the relationship.
However Eric goes off in a huff when he mistakenly believes that Polly has been making up to him only to get him to insure his hands with Bruce's company. The odd Mr. Willoughby helps to sort the tangle out, Eric suddenly displays a new toughness and life for him and Polly is all harmony again.

NOTES
The only thing the critics could do when faced with a thing like this was to shake their heads in disbelief, while the fans just stayed away.
'With each of David Niven's current Hollywood pictures the same question occurs: "What's going on? What on earth are they doing with that fellow's career?"' was the reaction of the *News of the World*.
'By far the unhappiest moments of the week were those spent at *A Kiss In the Dark*. Starring David Niven and Jane Wyman it proceeds to waste them both in one of the silliest and trashiest stories seen on the screen for many a long day.' That was the observation of the *Observer*.
This is one film that Niven should have turned down flat and made a fight of it. Apart from its triteness it is one of those nasty little pictures that illustrates Hollywood's philistine streak: in this case we see the genuine artist (the dedicated concert pianist) pulled from his pedestal and converted to the full vulgar life enjoyed by your average moron in the street—the worst sort of playing to what the industry used to call the cloth cap and muffler trade.

Enjoying 'the full vulgar life' with Jane Wyman. One flustered critic exclaimed 'What on earth are they doing with that fellow's career?'

THE ELUSIVE PIMPERNEL

(U.S. title: THE FIGHTING PIMPERNEL)

1949

London Films. *Producers/directors/writers:* Michael Powell and Emeric Pressburger—*from the first Pimpernel story by* Baroness Orczy. *Assistant Producer:* George R. Busby. *Camera:* Christopher Challis. *Designer:* Hein Heckroth. *Art:* Arthur Lawson. *Music:* Brian Eastdale. *Editors:* Charles Poulton, Red Law. *Running time:* 109 minutes. Technicolor.

CAST

David Niven . . . . *Sir Percy Blakeney*
Margaret Leighton . . . . . *Lady Blakeney*
Cyril Cusack . . . . *Chauvelin*
Jack Hawkins . . . . *Prince of Wales*
Arlette Marchal . . . . . . *Comtesse de Tournai*
Gerard Nery . . . . *Phillipe de Tournai*
Danielle Godet . . . . . . *Suzanne de Tournai*
Edmond Audran . . . . . . *Armand St. Just*
Charles Victor . . . . *Colonel Winterbotham*
Principal Gentlemen of the League
David Hutcheson . . . . . . *Lord Anthony Dewhurst*
Robert Coote . . . . *Sir Andrew Ffoulkes*
John Fitzgerald . . . . . . *Sir Michael Travers*
Patrick Macnee . . . . . . *Hon. John Bristow*
Terence Alexander . . . . . *Duke of Dorset*

STORY

The French revolution has reached the height of the Terror but many intended for execution are being snatched from the guillotine by the mysterious and elusive Scarlet Pimpernel.

Tracking him down on behalf of the French government is Citizen Chauvelin. He arrives in London as an official envoy and meets Lady Blakeney, wife of the fop Lord Blakeney but also a Frenchwoman and patriot. Chauvelin blackmails her into providing a clue to the Pimpernel. She does not know, of course, that she is betraying her own husband.

Sir Percy leaves for Le Mont St. Michel to resume his activities as the Pimpernel.

Lady Blakeney arrives there as well—intent on warning the Pimpernel of his danger. She is seized by Chauvelin, who has guessed Sir Percy's secret, and held as hostage. Blakeney barters himself for his wife. Imprisoned, he escapes. Chauvelin encircles the Mont

Back in costume with the Powell and Pressburger team in *The Elusive Pimpernel*. It couldn't survive memories of the earlier Leslie Howard version and didn't please Niven much, either.

Sir Percy Blakeney and cronies plotting the formation of the Pimpernel's league in a handy turkish bath.

Face to face with the dreaded Chauvelin (Cyril Cusack).

with soldiers to cut him off. But he is oddly unaware that when the tide comes in the Mont is surrounded by water. The Pimpernel and Lady Blakeney, radiant now she knows her husband is not an awful fop after all, sail away to England in the family yacht.

NOTES

David Niven was back in with the Powell and Pressburger team. Margaret Leighton, about the only member of the cast to emerge with any credit from *Bonnie Prince Charlie*, played Niven's leading lady once again. The film was notable on one minor level; at Carlton Mews David Niven acted his first scene on a London location.

The film was hammered by the Press but adored by the public, and a decent popular success was something the actor needed badly at this time.

The picture had a curious history. Although Powell and Pressburger were apparently in the business of making a simple costume drama, it seems they were aiming at something rather deeper and more satirical. The film was shown, to a chilly reception, at the Venice

Film Festival but it was quite a different, and more conventional, version that opened in London.

The critics greeted the movie like the mob in the Place de la Concorde welcoming the arrival of the latest tumbril.

'It must be one of the most expensively dull films we have made in this country for years. David Niven plays the Scarlet Pimpernel with the sheepish lack of enthusiasm of a tone deaf man called to sing solo in church. His companions lumber through their parts like schoolboys about to go down with mumps.'—*Daily Express*.

'Though David Niven and Margaret Leighton have their moments as Sir Percy and Lady Blakeney, the film will stand or fall on the crowd scenes and glimpses of French chateaux, Mont St. Michel and the Sussex downs all in richest Technicolor.'—*Daily Telegraph*.

'Film audiences are in danger of forgetting what a really accomplished actor Mr. Niven is. Here he makes his first embarrassed entrance like the dame in some nightmare pantomime.'—*The Times*.

A KISS FOR CORLISS

1949

Strand Productions. *Producer*: Colin Miller. *Director*: Richard Wallace. *Script*: Howard Dimsdale—*based on the character Corliss Archer created by* F. Hugh Herbert. *Camera*: Robert de Grasse. *Music*: Rudolph Polk. *Editor*: Frank Doyle. *Running time*: 88 minutes

CAST

Shirley Temple . . . . *Corliss Archer*
David Niven . . . . *Kenneth Maquis*
Tom Tully . . . . *Harry Archer*
Virginia Welles . . . . *Mildred*
Darryl Hickman . . . . *Dexter*
Robert Ellis . . . . *Raymond*
Richard Gaines . . . . *Taylor*
Kathryn Card . . . . *Louise*
Gloria Holden . . . . *Mrs. Archer*
Roy Roberts . . . . *Uncle George*

STORY

Kenneth Maquis, in the middle of his third divorce, is reputedly a notorious woman fancier. In fact, he's just ineffectual when it comes to fending off females. Harry Archer, a smart lawyer, is busy ensuring that the departing wife will get a handsome share of the loot. The lawyer's daughter Corliss has a rather different interest in Kenneth, as she sees him as a useful tool in a romantic scheme.

Corliss is having trouble with Dexter, her unenthusiastic beau. Aided by friend Mildred, Corliss concocts a fictitious romance—including a promise of marriage—with Kenneth, duly recorded in her diary, with the object of arousing Dexter's jealousy. The diary is entrusted to a local squirt, Raymond, with the certain knowledge the information will get back to Dexter.

A Kiss for Corliss (Shirley Temple) but a nasty back-hander for Niven.

Goldwyn lent him out for this twee, teenage comedy, says the actor, because he was plotting to get rid of him at the time.

It gets even further afield, as Raymond shows the racier passages to Kenneth. Kenneth visits the Archer home, denies nothing and offers to keep his 'promise' to marry Corliss, who is furious with this turn of events, as Kenneth intended. Then, after sufficient scandal has broken loose, he explains everything and peace is restored.

NOTES

This was a vehicle for the relatively ageing Shirley Temple, then 21-years-old and a mother, playing a 'bobby soxer'. David Niven took a back seat and welcomed it. He described the picture as 'a disastrous teenage potboiler'.

It was, however, a landmark of sorts, since it was the last picture he made for Sam Goldwyn, who'd had him under contract since his entry into pictures. He asked for his release and got it.

The public and the critics generally agreed with Niven's own assessment of the picture.

'Poor David Niven!' said the *Sunday Chronicle*. 'Only a really great star could save a picture in which he scarcely appears at all.' This was, presumably, intended as a compliment.

The Star was very kind in the circumstances: 'It's a tiny part for David Niven but ... he provides a few moments of quiet humour in a raucous picture...'

C. A. Lejeune, the *Observer* film critic and a great supporter of the actor, was driven to despairing verse on this occasion.

"I sometimes think that David Niven
Should not take *all* the parts he's given
While of the art of Shirley Temple
I, for the moment, have had ample.'

All things considered, Niven's expression of nausea is wholly understandable.

THE TOAST OF NEW ORLEANS

1950

M.G.M. *Producer*: Joe Pasternak. *Director*: Norman Taurog. *Script*: Sy Gomberg, George Wells. *Songs*: Nicholas Brodsky (*music*), Sammy Cahn (*lyrics*). *Camera*: William Snyder. *Art*: Cedric Gibbons, Daniel B. Cathcart. *Musical director*: George Stoll. *Editor*: Gene Ruggiero. *Running time*: 98 minutes. Technicolor.

CAST

Kathryn Grayson . . . . *Suzette Micheline*
Mario Lanza . . . . *Pepe Abellard Duvalle*
David Niven . . . . *Jacques Riboudeaux*
J. Carrol Naish . . . . *Nicky Duvalle*
James Mitchell . . . . *Pierre*
Richard Hageman . . . . . . *Maestro P. Trellini*
Clinton Sundberg . . . . *Oscar*
Sig Arno . . . . *Mayor*
Rita Moreno . . . . *Tina*
Romo Vincent . . . . *Manuello*

STORY

It is the ceremony of blessing the fishing fleet in the Bayou in the heart of America's deep South in the year 1905. Fisherman Pepe is more fascinated by the

Eating pizza with Mario Lanza. Better, perhaps, than eating humble pie for Sam Goldwyn.

Kisses for the leading lady . . . Kathryn Grayson.

The task of this film was to launch the Metro discovery Mario Lanza. Niven was along to add some charm, gain a few laughs and gracefully lose the lady.

Clowning with J. Carroll Naish.

Romance supervised by director Norman Taurog.

opera star Suzette Micheline, a guest at the ceremony, than navigating his boat, or rather his Uncle Nicky's boat. It gets out of line and misses the blessing. Nicky thinks this means misfortune and he's right. A storm destroys it.

Pepe sings a duet with the opera star at the festivities after the blessing, and attracts the admiration of Jacques Riboudeaux, manager of Suzette's opera company and enamoured of the star. He persuades Pepe to train for the opera and Pepe agrees so he can buy Uncle Nicky a new boat.

In New Orleans he studies singing and chats up Suzette. She rejects him. In despair he decides to quit the opera business.

Jacques, for whom love of art transcends all, persuades him to stay on, study to be a gentleman, and sue for Suzette's hand with elegance.

But it is the original oaf with the voice of gold that Suzette really admires. In the nick of time—or to be more exact in the middle of *Madam Butterfly*—he comes to his senses and takes her by storm.

NOTES

This was David Niven's inauspicious beginning as a freelance in a film made to launch M.G.M.'s new star Mario Lanza. It was hardly a part at all, he was a sort of spare minim at a bawling party. *The Star* newspaper put it in a nutshell. 'Kathryn Grayson and Mario Lanza spend about 97 minutes singing at each other.'

Clinch with Kathryn Grayson set up for a publicity still.

HAPPY GO LOVELY

1950

A.B.P.C. *Producer*: Marcel Helman. *Director*: Bruce Humberstone. *Script*: Val Guest—*from a story by* F. Damman and Dr. H. Rosenfield. *Music*: Mischa Spoliansky. *Camera*: Erwin Hellier. *Art*: John Howell. *Editor*: Bert Bates. *Running time*: 97 minutes. Technicolor.

CAST

David Niven	*B. G. Bruno*
Vera-Ellen	*Janet Jones*
Cesar Romero	*John Frost*
Bobby Howes	*Charlie*
Diane Hart	*Mae*
Gordon Jackson	*Paul Tracy*
Barbara Couper	*Madame Amanda*
Henry Hewitt	*Dodds*
Gladys Henson	*Mrs. Urquhart*
Hugh Dempster	*Bates*
Sandra Dorne	*Betty*
Joyce Carey	*Bruno's secretary*
John Laurie	*Jonskill*
Wylie Watson	*Stage Doorkeeper*
Joan Heal	*Phylis Gardiner*
Hector Ross	*Harold*
Ambrosine Phillpots	*Lady Martin*
Molly Urquhart	*Madame Amanda's assistant*

With Vera-Ellen at Elstree.

STORY

It is Edinburgh at Festival time but no cue for jollity for wise-cracking American producer John Frost, in town with a musical, *Frolics to You,* and a bag of debts.

His creditors give him 24 hours to raise some money before they foreclose. The leading lady quits and the other members of the cast threaten to do likewise.

Janet Jones, a chorus girl, is having a hard time staving off a creditor of her own and, being late for the theatre as a result, scrounges a lift in a plush chauffeur-driven car. It belongs to local millionaire greeting card king, B. G. Bruno.

Canny Frost assumes she is Bruno's girl and could become a source of funds. He promotes her to leading lady and local traders rush to supply her with clothes and other goodies—and hopefully send the bills to Bruno.

Bruno hastens to the theatre to investigate. Janet mistakes him for a local journalist and Bruno doesn't enlighten her. Bruno, much taken with the lady, puts up money for the show. But Janet, still under the impression he is the journalist, feels it morally incumbent upon her to expose the man—and his cheque—as a fraud. The police are called but Bruno's true identity as Bruno is soon established, romance prospers again and the show opens to rapturous acclaim.

NOTES

David Niven's third entry to the world of the lavish musical was little better fated than before. A.B.P.C. were obviously determined to make a Hollywood-style musical for export to America. In addition to the internationally known talents of David Niven, they included American stars Vera-Ellen and Cesar Romero. They even flew over Hollywood director Bruce Humberstone, whose films included Danny Kaye's *Wonder Man.*

The result however, was a poor imitation of the genuine article despite all the imported gloss. But David Niven worked hard to breathe life into the film and his work was rewarded.

'Mr. David Niven's charm helps enormously to blind one to the picture's defects...' said the *Spectator.*

The *Daily Mail,* after a cold reception to the picture, remarked: '... Yet Mr. Niven, back on top of his form

Always longing to break big into the American market, Associated British brought together Niven and Vera-Ellen and Cesar Romero with American director Bruce Humberstone to concoct an imitation American musical with a Scots setting.

As the man who made a million (with Vera-Ellen).

after a series of disappointing pictures, is an excellent light comedian. . . .'

'David Niven is rediscovered as a light comedian with a delightful portrayal of a bewildered businessman who finds himself involved in show business—and romance,' said the *Daily Mirror*.

Over in America, the *New York Times* wasn't particularly impressed. After detailing the plot Bosley Crowther remarked: 'Sounds pretty gosh awful, doesn't it? Well, in spots it is, especially when Mr. Niven, as the smitten young laird, acts cutely coy. But somehow, for all its hackneyed substance . . . there's a certain limpid charm.'

While shooting the picture Niven announced he'd gone into the writing business and was at work on a novel called *Round the Rugged Rocks*. He described it as a gentle satire on Americans and their habits, utilising some of his own experiences.

104

SOLDIERS THREE

1951

M.G.M. *Producer*: Pandro S. Berman. *Director*: Tay Garnett. *Script*: Marguerite Roberts, Tom Reed, Malcolm Stuart Boylan—*from the stories by* Rudyard Kipling. *Music*: Adolph Deutsch. *Camera*: William Mellor. *Art*: Cedric Gibbons, Malcolm Brown. *Editor*: Robert J. Kern. *Running time*: 92 minutes.

CAST

Stewart Granger	*Private Archibald Ackroyd*
Walter Pidgeon	*Colonel Brunswick*
David Niven	*Captain Pindenny*
Robert Newton	*Private Jock Sykes*
Cyril Cusack	*Private Dennis Malloy*
Greta Gynt	*Greenshaw*
Frank Allenby	*Colonel Groat*
Robert Coote	*Major Mercer*
Dan O' Herlihy	*Sergeant Murphy*
Michael Ansara	*Manik Rao*
Richard Hale	*Govind-Lal*
Patrick Whyte	*Major Robert Harrow*

STORY

Colonel Brunswick, in charge of the Rutlandshire Infantry on duty in India in the 1890s, is with his troops at Mirzabad in hopes of nabbing an anti-British Indian leader, Govind-Lal. But he is recalled to his base at Hyderalipore. He is joined by Colonel Groat and his 28th Dragoons. Groat, being the senior officer, takes command.

Apart from Indian agitators Brunswick has another burden to bear, three wild privates, Ackroyd, Sykes and Malloy. Will this disgraceful, drunken trio let the side down in the sight of Colonel Groat?

Captain Pindenny, Brunswick's adjutant, tries to save the situation by promoting Ackroyd to sergeant, thereby breaking up the partnership.

The plan works for a time but when battle breaks out the three become friends again.

Yet again in uniform with Robert Newton, Walter Pidgeon, Cyril Cusack and Stewart Granger in spoof Kipling.

105

On the carpet.

Trapped by attacking Indian troops.

Inspecting the extras.

Undignified return to camp.

A small group of troops is ordered to convoy an ammunition train to a deserted fort. Sykes and Molloy are included but Ackroyd is forbidden to join them. He deserts and finds them besieged by attacking tribesmen under the command of Manik Rao, a rebel against the authority of Govind-Lal, who turns out to be quite a goody.

Brunswick, disobeying Groat's orders, rides to the rescue. Ackroyd kills Manik Rao and the attack collapses. Brunswick, instead of a court martial, is made Brigadier-General. Ackroyd is 'punished' by being demoted to private and jubilantly rejoins his two comrades.

NOTES

This adventure story based—at some remove—on Rudyard Kipling won a medal from the *Daily Express* even before it started production. The *Express,* always sensitive where matters of national pride are involved,

'That's not funny, old man'—but Stewart Granger thinks it is.

praised M.G.M. for not only casting Britons as stars of the film—conveniently over-looking Walter Pigeon—but also flying over Britishers to take most of the rest of the parts.

'Those who attack Hollywood when it sends its stars to film in Britain should now keep quiet—including me,' concluded the writer.

M.G.M. may have transported the cast out of Britain in a blaze of publicity but they sneaked back the finished film in darkest secrecy. Listen to the *Daily Mail*. 'Arriving in the West End unheralded and unsung *Soldiers Three* in which Stewart Granger, Walter Pidgeon and David Niven are the three principal characters in a knock-about comedy.

'Kipling fans will probably have a fit but my guess is that it will have many people in fits of laughter.'

THE LADY SAYS NO!

1951

Stillman Productions. *Producers*: Frank Ross, John Stillman Jnr. *Director*: Frank Ross. *Script*: Robert Russell. *Camera*: James Wong Howe. *Editor*: George Amy. *Sound*: Fred Lau. *Music*: Emil Newman. *Running time*: 83 minutes.

CAST

Joan Caulfield . . . . *Dorinda Hatch*
David Niven . . . . *Bill Shelby*
James Robertson Justice . . . . *Uncle Matt*
Lenore Lonergan . . . . *Goldie*
Frances Bavier . . . . *Aunt Alice*
Peggy Maley . . . . *Midge*
Henry Jones . . . . *Potsy*
Jeff York . . . . *Goose*
George Davis . . . . *Bartender*
Robert Williams . . . . *General*
Mary Lawrence . . . . *Mary*

STORY

Photographer Bill Shelby is on the way to take magazine pictures of Dorinda Hatch, authoress of a sensational best seller, *The Lady Says No!*, warning women against men.

He picks up three hitch-hikers: Sergeant Potsy, his wife Goldie and her friend Midge.

At the Hatch residence the surprisingly attractive Dorinda agrees to pose for pictures on the beach—but then just pulls a face for the camera and strides away. That's what she thinks of men!

Bill sends Dorinda a copy of the grimacing picture he took of her, with the suggestion that it might make a great cover shot. He demands a kiss for the negative.

Dorinda surrenders and gives him the kiss—and then a crack on the jaw.

But Bill's efforts are paying off, and Dorinda is thawing. She goes to a bar the next evening, patronised by Bill and his hitch-hiker friends, looking for him, but she gets high. She makes a play for Potsy and rows with his wife. She is beastly to Bill who takes her home, warms her up on the porch and then drops her.

The next day Potsy has left his wife and moved in with Bill. Dorinda, conscience striken, reunites husband and wife and announces she is leaving home. But Bill catches her up and forces her car into the verge.

As Bill swings in for the fade-out kiss Dorinda tosses her book out of the car and its philosophy out of her life.

Thus, ignominiously, ends an early essay in Women's Lib.

NOTES

This is one of the black spots in the Niven career and it is kindest to pass over it quickly. The actor is curiously charmless, understandably as the part lacks any hint of charm.

'After some unfunny gadding about to prove that the male animal is not a beast, Mr. Niven, who has manoeuvred Miss Caulfield into seeing the light, makes this trenchant observation: "This went out with silent pictures!" Yes, indeed,' wrote the *New York Times*.

'Flatfooted comedy,' said the *Monthly Film Bulletin* of the British Film Institute curtly.

With Lenore Lonergan, Joan Caulfield and Frances Bavier.

APPOINTMENT WITH VENUS

(U.S. title: ISLAND RESCUE)

1951

British Film Makers. *Producer*: Betty E. Box. *Director*: Ralph Thomas. *Script*: Nicholas Phipps *from the novel by* Jerrard Tickell. *Associate Producer*: Peter Rogers. *Camera*: Ernest Seward. *Art*: George Provis. *Music*: Benjamin Frankel. *Editor*: Gerald Thomas. *Running time*: 89 minutes.

CAST

David Niven . . . . *Major Valentine Morland*
Glynis Johns . . . . *Nicola Fallaize*
Barry Jones . . . . *The Provost*
Kenneth More . . . . *Lionel Fallaize*
Noel Purcell . . . . *'Trawler' Langley*
George Coulouris . . . . . *Captain Weiss*
Bernard Lee . . . . *Brigadier*
Jeremy Spencer . . . . . . *George*
Patric Doonan . . . . . . *Kent*
George Benson . . . . . . *Senior Clerk*
Richard Wattis . . . . . . *Higher Executive*

STORY

Amorel, a minute scrap of land being the smallest of the Channel Islands (no bad mark if you've never heard of it, it's fictitious), is occupied by the Germans during the last war. The loss is born bravely by the British people who are more worried about rationing. But the Ministry of Agriculture is horrified, for Amorel houses about the nearest thing Britain had at the time to a secret weapon: Venus, a pedigree cow, in calf, and capable of mothering a line of champions.

The War Office co-operates with the Ministry of Agriculture and despatches an invasion force by submarine to rescue Venus.

In charge of the party is Major Morland, while aiding him is a pretty A.T.S. girl with local connections, Nicola, and 'Trawler' Langley, an old rascal with an unrivalled knowledge of the Amorel coast-line.

Led by Morland the islanders plan to rescue the cow from under the noses of the Germans. They have little

With the star of the title.

time. The German commandant, Captain Weiss, is an old cattleman himself and has already spotted the Venus potential and is arranging her shipment to Germany.

Everyone from the Provost down to Lionel, Nicola's painter cousin, who really doesn't want to be involved with the war at all, engage in a frenzied game of wit and outwit until Venus is finally liberated.

NOTES

It was becoming quite the thing in the film business that if you wanted a young dashing, romantic and light-hearted army officer, send for Niven. Those early days when he actually was a young army officer and, by his own account, dashing, romantic and light-hearted, were paying off, it seemed.

The idea of this film, shot on location in Sark, was a peculiarly British conception and not likely to travel well. It certainly baffled the *New Yorker*'s man.

'*Island Rescue,* an English film, sets out to be a farce and then gets so earnest about itself that it winds up as a kind of blurred melodrama. Since the liberation of a well bred cow struck me as being too elfin a notion, I may have missed some of the humour.'

Time said: 'The humour ... sometimes wears a bit thin. But the picture is zestfully acted.'

The Times noted that the picture was combining

With Glynis Johns.

comedy with adventure. 'Always a tricky mixture for a film to handle, but *Appointment With Venus* manages it skilfully enough even if the joke itself is a trifle faded and there is something a little half-hearted in the air of conviction it brings to the narrative. Still, it is pleasant to watch Mr. Niven going about his work—although that is too stern a word—of being nonchalant as he is gifted, as gay as he is determined, a twentieth-century Pimpernel with an aristocrat of a cow to snatch from under the noses of the enemy.'

THE MOON IS BLUE

1953

A Preminger–Herbert Production. *Producers*: Otto Preminger, F. Hugh Herbert. *Director*: Otto Preminger. *Script*: F. Hugh Herbert—*from his play.* *Camera*: Ernest Laszlo. *Music*: Hershel Burke Gilbert. *Art*: Nicolei Remisoff. *Editors*: Louise R. Loeffler, Otto Ludwig. *Running time*: 97 minutes.

CAST

William Holden . . . . *Donald Gresham*
David Niven. . . . . *David Slater*
Maggie McNamara . . . . *Patty O' Neill*
Tom Tully. . . . . *Michael O' Neill*
Dawn Addams . . . . *Cynthia Slater*
Fortunio Bonanova . . . . *Television singer*
Gregory Ratoff . . . . *Taxi Driver*

STORY

Patty O'Neill is a budding TV actress with a promiscuous line in patter but strict adherence to middle-class morality when it comes to performance. She is picked up on the top of the Empire State Building by successful architect Donald Gresham and accepts his invitation to dinner.

They call in at his apartment on their way to dine but as Patty claims to be a good cook they decide to eat there. While Donald is out buying food former girl friend Cynthia drops in for a brief stay, as does her father David, a suave and seasoned trapper of wide-eyed young ladies. Patty invites him to stay to dinner. David proposes marriage and offers her 600 dollars,

The moment most actors dread . . . face to face with Preminger.

as a no-strings gift, of course. She accepts the gift readily but rejects the offer and is caught by Donald bestowing a grateful kiss upon David. This is annoying enough, but worse follows when Patty's father storms into the apartment and knocks him cold.

The romance seems damaged beyond repair but the next day both parties are drawn to the top of the Empire State to meet once again—and this time Donald proposes marriage.

NOTES

David Niven's career seemed on the road to extinction at this time. His break-up with Goldwyn had not been cordial and the Goldwyn office maliciously put it about that Niven had been fired. His pictures since the parting hadn't helped his reputation in the film capital much either.

Then Otto Preminger came to the star's rescue with this part. Being rescued by Otto Preminger was rather like being snatched from drowning by King Kong. He enjoyed a reputation for tyranny on the set, striking terror into the hearts of actors and technicians alike. But David Niven emerged from the ordeal quite unscathed and deeply grateful to Preminger for casting him in defiance of Hollywood's baleful animosity. United Artists had described him as 'washed up' and advised Preminger 'get somebody else'.

The Moon is Blue outraged many at the time by using such words as 'seduce' and 'virgin'. It was condemned by the Catholic Church and banned by the censor. Aided by the distributors, United Artists, Preminger defied the ban and released the film, the first time the American film censor had been so defied.

It was Preminger's first film as an independent producer, having formed a company with the playwright, F. Hugh Herbert, to make the picture after directing the original stage play. The scandalous publicity guaranteed an enormous success; a good send-off into independence for Preminger and a Heaven-sent boost for Niven. It gained him few good reviews in Britain, however, but won him the Golden Globe Award from the Foreign Press Association for the best comedy performance of the year.

Over here, *Kine Weekly* was kindly: 'David Niven completely disarms'.

Variety said: 'Niven's middle-aged playboy is mighty fancy play-acting.'

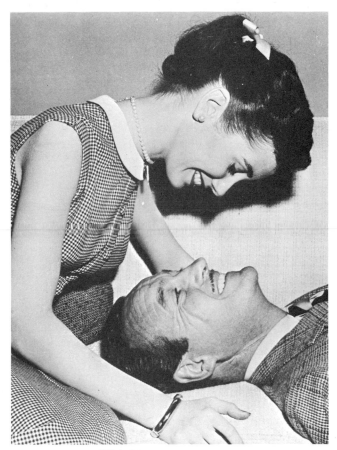

With Maggie McNamara.

With William Holden.

The picture infuriated the critics but proved a useful vehicle for Niven.

THE LOVE LOTTERY

1953

Ealing Studios. *Producer*: Monja Danischewsky. *Director*: Charles Crichton. *Script*: Harry Kurnitz. *Camera*: Douglas Slocombe. *Music*: Benjamin Frankel. *Design*: Tom Morahan. *Editor*: Seth Holt. *Running time*: 89 minutes. Technicolor.

CAST

David Niven . . . . *Rex Allerton*
Peggy Cummins . . . . *Sally*
Anne Vernon . . . . *Jane*
Herbert Lom . . . . *Amico*
Charles Victor . . . . *Jennings*
Gordon Jackson . . . . *Ralph*
Felix Aylmer . . . . *Winant*
Hugh McDermott . . . . *Rodney Wheeler*
Stanley Maxted . . . . *Stanton*
June Clyde . . . . *Viola*
John Chandos . . . . *Gulliver Kee*
Gabriella Blunt . . . . *Doreen*
Hattie Jacques . . . . *Chambermaid*

STORY

Actor Rex Allerton is No. 2 star at his Hollywood studio. No. 1 star is Fang, the wonder dog. The pressures of fame are weighing heavily upon Rex. He even has recurring dreams in which he is torn apart by ravening fans.

He attempts a rebellion but it peters out. In a fatefully blasé moment, when a columnist suggests that the prize in a competition for women might be a week for the winner with him in Hollywood, Rex answers: 'I will marry her.' It's meant as a joke but taken up seriously.

Smooth operator Amico, head of the International Syndicate of Computation, gets in on the act. He uses glamorous Jane to ensure that Rex is trapped into keeping his promise and the 'Love Lottery' is launched. But Jane and Rex have fallen in love and announce their engagement.

His world-wide feminine fans, led by starry-eyed Sally in Britain, are furious and even bring a mass breach

With Herbert Lom.

of promise suit that fails. The lottery goes ahead with Rex and Jane buying all the tickets they can lay their hands on. But Sally wins.

Sally, however, finds that the super-star is not so super in real life; quite a gentle, mixed up sort of man, a bit like the fiancé she ditched back home. The road is clear for Jane to undo all the bad work and claim Rex for herself.

NOTES

Ealing Studios, the cradle of British film comedy, had become over-involved with the 'shabby mac' dramas of the period and critics welcomed them back to fun-land with this picture, even if they had quite a few reservations.

They liked the British spoofing of Hollywood and they admired some of the set-pieces in the best Ealing man-ner—the film-star's dream sequence, for instance—and they all applauded David Niven.

'The cinema seldom goes far wrong when it decides to laugh at itself. The new Ealing picture does this with gusto. David Niven has his best part for a long time and rises splendidly to the occasion.'—*Daily Mail*.

'David Niven is just right . . . .'—*Daily Express*.

The *Observer* found the film old fashioned and the screenplay by Hollywood scriptwriter Harry Kurnitz untidy, but wrote: 'It has a charming and talented heroine in the person of Anne Vernon and two of my favourite experts in make-believe, David Niven and Herbert Lom, have leading parts.'

HAPPY EVER AFTER

(U.S. title: TONIGHT'S THE NIGHT)

1954

A Mario Zampi Production for A.B.P.C. *Producer/director*: Mario Zampi. *Script*: Jack Davies, Michael Pertwee—*additional dialogue by* L. A. G. Strong. *Camera*: Stanley Pavey. *Art*: Ivan King. *Music*: Stanley Black. *Running time*: 84 minutes. Technicolor.

CAST

David Niven . . . . *Jasper O'Leary*
Yvonne de Carlo . . . . *Serena McGlusky*
Barry Fitzgerald . . . . *Thady O'Heggarty*
George Cole . . . . *Terence*
A. E. Matthews . . . . *General O'Leary*
Noelle Middleton . . . . *Kathy McGlusky*
Robert Urquhart . . . . *Michael Flynn*
Michael Shepley . . . . *Major McGlusky*
Joseph Tomelty . . . . *Dooley*

STORY

When the squire of Rathbarney in Ireland, General O'Leary, is killed he is succeeded by a distant and shady relative, Jasper O'Leary. He intends to squeeze the estate dry. He prohibits poaching, collects debts, ejects defaulting tenants and does all the things long neglected by a line of lovable squires.

The villagers are dumbfounded, or as dumbfounded as Irish villagers could ever be, and decide on a desperate measure: they will murder the new squire. Only Serena McGlusky, a widow very little better than she ought to be, fancies the man.

The various conspiracies of the villagers to polish off Jasper go comically wrong but finally their traditional way of life, and Jasper's skin, are saved when a new will is unearthed naming a well-loved local citizen as squire should Jasper prove unpopular.

With Yvonne de Carlo.

NOTES

This comedy by Mario Zampi who catered for the middle-market filmgoer was vociferously abused by the critics although it was a harmless, and occasionally, very funny, comedy of stage Irish characters. But then this was before we were inundated with similarly contrived, knockabout situation comedies of a tenth of its value in countless TV series. We knew not the value we had.

Many commentators thought Niven mis-cast as a 'heavy' although this was ascribing too much weight, if one may use the word, to a character who was essentially a pantomine villain we were expected to hiss. Admittedly, Niven's portrayal reminded one of the sort of rather supercilious junior officers who abound in the Army and who certainly must have been familiar figures to Niven in his own Army days,

Niven's character was essentially a pantomime villain.

rather than the fruitier bounder we might have expected.

'Niven is wasted in this unsympathetic role,' said the American *Saturday Review*.

'Mr. Niven, who has his limitations outside light comedy, seems most unhappy in this part,' said the *Evening News*.

But David had his supporters. 'David Niven has an unusual role—the bad boy—in *Happy Ever After*. He carries it off surprisingly well,' said the *Daily Mirror*.

'It's not for me,' said the *Sunday Graphic*, 'but I admired the dignity of David Niven in trying circumstances.'

The reviewer of the *Daily Mail* was one of the few who liked the picture.

'Almost everyone on hand is a flagrantly unashamed bog character except A. E. Matthews, who dominates a wonderful opening sequence, Yvonne de Carlo, whose attractions transcend race, religion or geography, and Mr. Niven.'

Mixed reviews!

118

CARRINGTON V.C.

(U.S. title: COURT MARTIAL)

1954

Romulus. *Producer*: Teddy Baird. *Director*: Anthony Asquith. *Script*: John Hunter—*from the play by Dorothy and Campbell Christie. Camera*: Desmond Dickenson. *Editor*: Ralph Kemplen. *Running time*: 105 minutes.

CAST

David Niven . . . . *Major Carrington V.C.*
Margaret Leighton . . . . . *Valerie*
Noelle Middleton . . . . . . *Captain Alison Graham*
Laurence Naismith . . . . . *Major Panton*
Clive Morton . . . . *Lt. Col. Huxford*
Mark Dignam . . . . *The Prosecutor*
Allan Cuthbertson . . . . . *Lt. Col. Henniker*
Victor Maddern . . . . *Sgt. Owen*
John Glyn-Jones . . . . . . *Evans*
Raymond Francis . . . . . *Major Mitchell*
Geoffrey Keen . . . . *The President*
Maurice Denham . . . . . . *Lt. Col. Reeve*
Michael Bates . . . . *Major Broke-Smith*

STORY

Major 'Cooper' Carrington is in a tight corner: the War Office owe him £200 but the authority to pay it is still marching at a funeral pace through a procession of War Office 'out' trays. In the meantime Valerie, his spoilt and neurotic wife, is demanding £100 to pay bills. The Major is broke.

He tries to get help from his C.O., Lt. Col. Henniker, but Henniker, a spiteful and petty man, won't help. He is jealous of Carrington's fine war record and his popularity.

Carrington, in desperation, threatens to take the money from the Battery safe. Henniker confines him to camp and warns him that a court-martial will follow if he carries out his threat. Carrington takes £125 from the safe; £100 he sends to his wife and £25 he bets on a horse he is riding that day in the Royal Artillery Golden Cup, leaving the camp to do so.

Alison Graham, a W.R.A.C. officer, who keeps more than a motherly eye on Carrington, tries to help. But the result is she is caught in his room at night, which makes matters worse.

Henniker carries out his threat. Carrington is court-martialled on three counts: misappropriation of the money, absence without leave and having a W.R.A.C. officer in his room.

Carrington conducts his own case but his wife—sensing an affair—lets him down and Henniker denies Carrington had warned him of his intention to take an 'advance' from the company safe.

The officer is found guilty and dismissed from the Army. He is saved from this fate when a camp telephonist admits to listening in to a telephone conversation that proves Carrington told the truth.

With Margaret Leighton.

On trial.

NOTES

Once again Niven was in a film that ran into trouble with the Hollywood censors; but this time the film was British and a remarkably good one. It was the sympathetic view taken by the film towards Carrington's relationship with the W.R.A.C officer, while wilting under the strain of an oppressive lawful wife, that upset the American Production Code Administration. They banned it because no one was permitted to exhibit 'extra-marital relationships in a casual or condoning manner', but if limited to the private lives of baddies or used to raise hysterical laughs it was all right.

But the film was the best all-round success for Niven over some five or six pretty barren years. He had the advantage of the impeccable Anthony Asquith as director; a character the very antithesis of his last maestro in Hollywood, Otto Preminger. Asquith, a tiny, gentle, gnome-like man, made virtually no concessions to the stock image of the film director, except perhaps for his colourful scarves. His manner was so quiet and his results with actors so remarkable that one can only suspect that he had some magical quality for communicating almost without words.

Time, while enjoying the film, took a dig at the happy ending. 'However, not even the law-abiding British can let the hero suffer such a wrong at the box-office so a twist ending should make all Niven fans happy.'

The British were content to praise the film and spare the carping.

'Mr. David Niven is very good in this part,' said the *Financial Times,* 'having just the spontaneous decency of reaction and the temperamental mixture of lightness and dash of which heroes are made.'

'One of the most satisfactory British pictures that has come up during the past years,' said *Time and Tide.* 'In a cast in which everyone deserves an honourable mention David Niven, Victor Maddern and Geoffrey Keen stand out.'

'David Niven, who seems on the face of it to be miscast for a semi-tragic role, gives one of the best performances of his career,' said the *Spectator.*

The *News of the World* was quite overcome. 'Not only has it a great and moving quality but it sends you away feeling proud of Britain's film-makers and actors . . . and of the British Army.'

The *Observer* was informative. 'When it was announced that David Niven was to play the title role in *Carrington V.C.* several people commented on the oddity of the casting. It is not really odd, for the part was written for him. The authors, Dorothy and Campbell Christie, "saw" their soldier hero as a man like Niven.

'Niven, one should remember, has not always been a light comedian, many people will be glad to reencounter the graver actor of *The Dawn Patrol.*'

With Noelle Middleton and Raymond Francis.

THE KING'S THIEF

1955

M.G.M. *Producer*: Edwin H. Knopf. *Director*: Robert Z. Leonard. *Script*: Christopher Knopf *from a story by* Robert Hardy Andrews. *Camera*: Robert Planck. *Music*: Miklos Rozsa. *Editor*: John McSweeney. *Running time*: 79 minutes. Eastmancolor/Cinemascope.

CAST

Ann Blyth . . . . *Lady Mary*
Edmund Purdom . . . . *Michael Dermott*
David Niven . . . . *Duke of Brampton*
George Sanders . . . . *Charles II*
Roger Moore . . . . *Jack*
John Dehner . . . . *Captain Herrick*
Sean McClory . . . . *Sheldon*
Tudor Owen . . . . *Simon*
Melville Cooper . . . . *Henry Wynch*
Alan Mowbray . . . . *Sir Gilbert Talbot*
Rhys Williams . . . . *Turnkey*

STORY

The Duke of Brampton, a black-hearted villain, enjoys the confidence of Charles II and uses his position to scheme against and ensnare as alleged traitors many nobles of impeccable probity: they lose their heads and the Duke snatches their estates. His ultimate aim is to overthrow the king, no less, and usurp his throne. His plans are jeopardised when a 'black' book of names of his victims—and potential victims—falls into the hands of Michael Dermott, a former officer and gentleman turned highwayman.

But Brampton captures Dermott and regains the incriminating book. Dermott is spirited out of jail with the help of Lady Mary, a beauty whose father had been betrayed by Brampton.

Dermott and Lady Mary determine upon an audacious ploy. They will steal the crown jewels and then use them as a bargaining point for securing a royal audience and unmasking the evil duke.

David Niven as villain (and looking remarkably like Basil Rathbone whose sort of part it was) with hero Edmund Purdom and George Sanders as Charles II.

With Edmund Purdom and Ann Blyth.

They nearly pull off the daring raid but are surprised by Brampton and his men accompanied by the King. Dermott engaged Brampton in a duel, disarms him and, at sword-point, forces him to confess his villainy.

NOTES
This film was certainly one of a number of low points in Niven's new career as a freelance actor. It was not just that he was cast as a villain, that's happened before, but that he was cast as a charmless, silly villain in one of those Hollywood historical charades that are redeemed for British cinemagoers only by the hilarious ineptitude of the script.
'I've heard the name some place,' says Edmund Pur-

dom. And a typical British 17th-century wench remarks, 'I've done thy shirt.'
'Hard work by Edmund Purdom, Ann Blyth, George Sanders and David Niven cannot whip any excitement or vestige of authenticity into this Restoration drama,' said the *Evening News*. 'Niven, smothered in ringlets, plots madly to kill all the king's supporters. I thought Niven looked happy only when he was arrested.'
'It would be hard to find an actor less suited to the part of a seventeenth-century villain than David Niven,' snapped the *Spectator*.
Variety produced about the kindest words: '*The King's Thief* proves to be a fairly diverting period piece that should exert a mild interest at the whickets.'

With Ann Blyth.

In costume ... but out of character.

Swashbuckler Niven in training for the part with Jean Heremans, a former Olympics champion and often in demand for such duties.

THE BIRDS AND THE BEES

1956

Gomalco Productions. *Producer*: Paul Jones. *Director*: Norman Taurog. *Script*: Sidney Sheldon, Preston Sturges—*based on a story by* Monckton Hoffe. *Musical numbers staged by*: Nick Castle. *New songs*: Harry Warren, Mack David. *Camera*: Daniel L. Fapp. *Music*: Walter Scharf. *Editor*: Archie Marshek. *Costumes*: Edith Head. *Running time*: 94 minutes. Technicolor/Vistavision.

CAST

George Gobel . . . . *George Hamilton*
Mitzi Gaynor . . . . *Jean Harris*
David Niven . . . . *Colonel Harris*
Reginald Gardiner . . . . *Gerald*
Harry Bellaver . . . . *Marty Kennedy*
Fred Clark . . . . *Horace Hamilton*
Margery Maude . . . . *Mrs. Hamilton*
Hans Conreid . . . . *Frenchy*
Mary Treen . . . . *Mrs. Burnside*
Peggy Moffatt . . . . *Miss Penny*
Rex Evans . . . . *Burrows*

STORY

George Hamilton, the shy and bumbling son of Horace, a tough old meat-packing tycoon, is returning from an African safari, under the watchful eye of his bodyguard-cum-valet, Marty, when he meets a trio of shipboard cardsharpers. They mark him down at once as a valuable pigeon.

Chief crook Colonel Harris sets his daughter Jean to ensnare simple George with the approval of his accomplice, Gerald. The planned fleece gets under way with only one snag, since Jean falls for her victim.

The effect of romance on George is to smarten up his personality no end, but Marty breaks up everything by exposing the trio.

Colonel Harris is unwilling to lose so profitable a proposition and the three pursue George—slipped back, alas, to his old pre-romance, twitish self—to the lavish Hamilton family mansion.

They bum an invitation pretending to be French nobles, and Jean becomes a thinly disguised Louise. George, noting the resemblance to his old love, courts, wins and marries her. Joy is short-lived, as Marty exposes the trio again. It's back to the ship, bound for Africa, for George. Waiting for him aboard is Jean, but this time she aims to wheedle nothing out of him but love.

NOTES

This was a vehicle to launch into pictures the big TV hit of the day, George Gobel, as the gormless hero galvanised by love. It didn't do much for Gobel, and Niven, as Colonel Harris, gave the performance of the picture as a genial, gentle and, of course, charming cad.

The fact that it was a re-make of Preston Sturges's brilliant comedy, *The Lady Eve*, damned it in the eyes of most critics even before it hit the screen. While not a patch on the original it was not half as bad as many painted it.

'Mitzi Gaynor is the girl and David Niven is likeable but unscrupulous; both of them (he especially) are very capable of being funny given just a little chance. Here they are served by a woefully predictable, unsurprising script,' said the *Manchester Guardian*.

Time took the film to task on different grounds: '*The Birds and the Bees* abets the growing suspicion that Hollywood is engaged in a Machiavellian plot to destroy television by sabotaging TV's best comics.'

But it was not a total verbal lashing. 'A very smooth comedy' (*News of the World*), 'an amusing piece of nonsense' (*Daily Mail*), 'a witty film' (*Daily Herald*).

With Mitzi Gaynor.

AROUND THE WORLD IN EIGHTY DAYS

1956

London Films–Michael Todd Productions. *Producer*: Michael Todd. *Director*: Michael Anderson. *Script*: James Poe, John Farrow, S. J. Perelman—*from the novel by* Jules Verne. *Music*: Victor Young. *Costumes*: Miles White. *Choreography*: Paul Godkin. *Art*: James Sullivan, Ken Adam. *Camera*: Lionel Lindon. *Foreign locations director*: Kevin McClory. *Running time*: 176 minutes. Eastmancolor/Todd-AO.

CAST

David Niven	*Phileas Fogg*
Cantinflas	*Passepartout*
Robert Newton	*Mr. Fix*
Shirley MacLaine	*Princess Aouda*
Charles Boyer	*Monsieur Gasse*
Ronald Colman	*Railway official*
Noel Coward	*Roland Hesketh-Baggott*
Marlene Dietrich	*Saloon keeper*
Fernandel	*Paris coachman*
John Gielgud	*Foster*
Hermione Gingold	*Pub lady*
Trevor Howard	*Fallentin*
Buster Keaton	*Tram conductor*
Peter Lorre	*Japanese steward*
Victor McLaglen	*Helmsman*
John Mills	*London cabby*
Frank Sinatra	*Saloon musician*

and many more stars in supporting parts.

STORY

The adventurous and daring Phileas Fogg claims he could circumnavigate the globe in only eighty days and accepts a bet of £20,000, put up by sceptical cronies at the Reform Club in St. James's, that he can't do it.

Phileas wastes no time in putting his boast to the test. That night he and his valet, Passepartout, take the boat train to Paris on the first leg of their journey, equipped with changes of shirt and socks and a carpetbag full of money.

With Phileas endlessly consulting his watch and confronted with every imaginable delaying phenomena

With Shirley MacLaine.

Aloft with Cantinflas.

the pair battle around the world and through a succession of spectacular adventures, a journey by balloon, a train ride through the Wild West accompanied by attacking Indians and an escape from angry tribesmen in India among them. It is in India that he rescues Aouda, an Indian Princess about to be burnt alive on the funeral pyre of her dead husband. He takes her under his wing as he races along.

In the course of the journey he encounters Inspector Fix of the Yard who is tracking him under the impression that Fogg is an escaping bank robber. He stays on his tail only awaiting a warrant from England for Fogg's arrest.

Fogg gets back to Liverpool and is about to board the train to London, in ample time to win the bet, when Fix arrests him. He is soon proved innocent and released—but time has fled and the bet seems lost.

Reconciled to ruin, Fogg is comforted by Aouda, and they plan to marry. Then Passepartout realises that all is not lost, as they had gained a day by international time changes. It is but a smart dash to the Reform Club and the wager is formally won.

NOTES

David Niven's introduction to the film version of Jules Verne's *Around the World in Eighty Days* was a typically brusque and laconic telephone call from entrepreneur Mike Todd demanding his presence. Fortunately the actor obeyed the summons. Jules Verne had supplied the cinema with a number of subjects but never did he get such lavish treatment.

It was, trumpeted the publicity department with some justification, the most elaborate epic of all time. 'The

With star 'bit player' Fernandel.

most stars—50. The most people ever photographed in world wide locations—68,984 in 13 different countries. The most miles travelled to make a film—4 million air passenger miles. The most sets ever used—140 actual locations, stages of 6 Hollywood studios, studios in England, Hong Kong and Japan. The most camera set-ups ever used—2,000. The most costumes ever designed, made or rented—74,685. The most assistant directors ever employed on a single picture.' Clearly, they also had one of Hollywood's best mathematicians. The picture with the mostest cost six million dollars, nearly equalled the record take of *Gone With the Wind* and won the year's Best Picture Oscar. Remarkably David Niven was not buried under this sumptuous avalanche of spectacle, and netted as many good reviews as the special effects.

'David Niven's quite essentially English gentleman is never in any danger of disappearing: he dominates even this gigantic screen with as fine a performance as he has given us for many a long year,' said the *Manchester Guardian*.

'David Niven is superb,' said the *Financial Times*. 'His hauteur never varies a fraction but beneath it powerful forces can be seen at work: his finest moment comes when he dismisses a troublesome detective, "What is more, sir, you play a very bad game of whist".'

'David Niven as the imperturbable traveller could hardly be bettered,' said the *Sunday Times*.

The *New York Post* found it 'a bubble of delight', *Time* decided '... the star of stars is the famous Mexican Cantinflas'. The vaunted Cantinflas, however, unlike Niven, soon disappeared from the international cinema scene.

With old friends of the Hollywood British colony: Cedric Hardwicke and Ronald Colman.

Niven as navigator ... his career on the right course.

129

A spectacular Red Indian attack on this train was just one of the hazards of the journey and one of the highlights of the film.

Delayed by the Salvation Army.

Always the true English gentleman.

Two more illustrious bit players: Marlene Dietrich and Frank Sinatra.

THE LITTLE HUT

1956

Herbson, Mark Robson and F. Hugh Herbert for M.G.M. *Producers*: F. Hugh Herbert, Mark Robson. *Director*: Mark Robson. *Script*: F. Hugh Herbert— *from the play by* Andre Roussin *and English adaptation by* Nancy Mitford. *Camera*: F. A. Young. *Editor*: Ernest Walter. *Music*: Robert Farnon. *Art*: Elliot Scott. *Running time*: 90 minutes. Eastmancolor.

CAST

Ava Gardner . . . . . . *Susan, Lady Ashlow*
Stewart Granger . . . . *Sir Philip Ashlow*
David Niven . . . . . . *Henry Brittingham-Brett*
Walter Chiari . . . . . *Mario*
Finlay Currie . . . . . *The Rev. Brittingham-Brett*
Jean Cadell . . . . . . *Mrs. Brittingham-Brett*
Jack Lambert . . . . . *Captain McWade*
Henry Oscar . . . . . . *Mr. Trollope*
Viola Lyel . . . . *Miss Edwards*
Jaron Yaltan . . . . . . *Indian*

STORY

Lady Ashlow, her husband Sir Philip and family friend, Henry Brittingham-Brett, are ship-wrecked and marooned on a dulcet tropical island; a sort of Swiss Family the Hon. Robinson.

Henry, a former boy-friend of Susan Ashlow, sees the opportunity not as one for labour and prayer but as a chance to renew an old liaison. He implies to Sir Philip that he and Susan have been secret lovers for years and wouldn't it be reasonable to indulge in a little wife-swapping? Susan, a long-time neglected wife, agrees to the idea because she hopes it will arouse her husband's jealousy and his dormant affections.

As it happens Sir Philip goes so far as to arrange a 'divorce ceremony' and hands his wife over to Henry. This back-fires on Henry who finds himself in the position of husband and Philip in the more romantic situation of lover. This triangle is made truly square when Mario, the handsome ship's chef, who also

With Ava Gardner and Stewart Granger.

Director Mark Robson and scriptwriter F. Hugh Herbert with Niven and Granger. Not the finest hour for any of them.

The stars all at sea.

escapes the wreck, turns up to stake his claim.

When the party are rescued and returned home the island divorce is declared illegal, to the delight of Sir Philip and her ladyship who have been transformed back into a happy family with a baby on the way.

NOTES

After the glamorous globe trotting in the making of *Around the World in Eighty Days* this was very much an economy trip although filming took place in Britain (briefly), Jamaica and Cinecitta Studios, Rome for some air-conditioned jungle scenes; the reported cost was £600,000.

The film's reception was enough to make any actor wish he'd stayed at home. This was 1956 and despite an X certificate the degree of permissiveness required before the risqué suggestions of a very naughty French play would be allowed on the screen had not yet reached the cinema.

'The picture is full of witless and double entendres and the central trio, Stewart Granger, David Niven and Ava Gardner, never comes into any comprehensible focus,' said the *New Yorker*.

'It is so busy giving sops to the censor that its triangulation becomes embarrassing,' said the *Spectator*.

'It's merely an unskilled Hollywood parody of some presumed British types and patterns of behaviour,' said the *Observer*.

On the popular front the *Daily Mirror* liked it ('... a highly amusing, harmless little film ...') but *The People* didn't ('... lacking the original wit and polish...').

The *Manchester Guardian* found it devoid of wit and grace but added: 'For the little that survives Mr. Niven, chiefly, deserves thanks.'

And said the *Daily Sketch*: 'David Niven—the one saving grace of *The Little Hut*.'

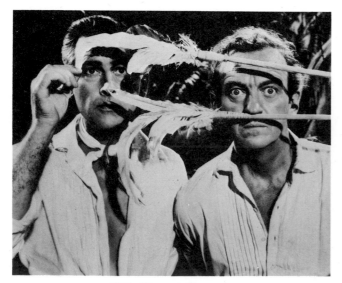

With Stewart Granger.

136

Tropical high jinks with Ava Gardner.

THE SILKEN AFFAIR

1956

Dragon Films. *Producers*: Douglas Fairbanks, Fred Feldkamp. *Director*: Roy Kellino. *Script*: Robert Lewis Taylor—*from a story by* John McCarten. *Camera*: Gilbert Taylor. *Editor*: Richard Best. *Art*: Paul Sheriff. *Running time*: 96 minutes.

CAST

David Niven . . . . *Roger Tweakham*
Genevieve Page . . . . *Ilsa Gerard*
Ronald Squire . . . . *Marberry*
Beatrice Straight . . . . *Theora*
Wilfred Hyde White . . . . *Sir Horace Hogg*
Howard Marion-Crawford . . . . . *Baggott*
Dorothy Alison . . . . *Mrs. Tweakham*
Richard Wattis . . . . *Worthington*
Miles Malleson . . . . *Mr. Blucher*
Joan Sims . . . . *Lady Barber*
Irene Handl . . . . *Receptionist*
Charles Carson . . . . *Judge*

STORY

Roger Tweakham is an ace accountant but the deuce of a dull fellow—hardly notices his wife—a slave to office routine but with a romantic heart buried beneath the book work.

Inspired by a chance meeting with a dazzling French girl, Ilsa, he does an odd thing when checking the accounts of Marberry—a genial silk stocking manufacturer, on the edge of ruin—he cooks the figures to show the old chap is booming.

At his next call, Gossamer Vogue, rivals of Marberry, he reverses the process—transforming Gossamer Vogue from a prosperous business to a dud concern, on paper. He just can't stand the firm's director.

Ilsa finds his quixotic behaviour delightful but Roger is already repenting. Ilsa introduces him to financial genius Sir Horace Hogg; his solution: Roger must hastily buy up all G. V.'s falling shares. But Marberry, anxious to extend his firm further, is to have his books checked, so Roger starts buying his shares as well.

He is discovered and sent for trial. Justice being in a romantic mood too, he is let off with a fine. Ilsa is left behind as a sweet memory and Roger, a changed man, returns to his wife capable of making domestic life balance at last.

NOTES

This film was based on an original story by John McCarten, film critic of the *New Yorker,* and if you want to see dog eat dog you should read the collected reviews of this picture. Hosts of Mr. McCarten's colleagues cheerfully chopped it to shreds.

With Genevieve Page.

Bowler-hatted as an accountant with a heart of gold.

With wily Wilfrid Hyde White.

'Mr. Niven, giving an impeccable, and at times, brilliant comic performance, is nevertheless, by the end, as completely submerged in fatuity as his dearest enemy could wish,' said the *Sunday Express*. David Niven, as so often happened, is praised in the same breath as his film is destroyed.

In view of the picture's theme what did the *Financial Times* have to say?

'For a while we seem to be on the verge of that comedy which has been crying out to be written for so long, about the more ingenious ramifications of tax evasion and expense accounting. But then, unfortunately, the film gets bogged down with an excess of shaggy dog jokes and puerile situations.'

Critics found *The Silken Affair* a thing of rags and patches, but all praised Niven.

The *Daily Telegraph* was kind. 'Agreeable, civilised entertainment with enough style and wit to atone for the bits that don't come off.' So was the *Daily Mail*. 'Mr. Niven, who has not always been well served in his recent films, has a chance in this one to show that when he is properly suited he has no equal in his own field of precise, polished comedy.'

Even the *Financial Times* softened when referring to the star: 'Mr. Niven remains one of the most accomplished light comedians in the business.'

'That it has a handful of funny moments cannot be denied,' concedes the *Observer,* 'and David Niven, whose charm is lethal, makes the most of them.'

And just listen to *Time and Tide*. 'In the tradition of gentlemanly foolishness which English farce and P. G. Wodehouse have in common (and of which neither has any reason to feel ashamed) David Niven is just about the best living exponent.'

With that renowned scene-stealer Richard Wattis.

OH MEN! OH WOMEN!

1957

20th-Century Fox. *Producer/director/script*: Nunnally Johnson. *Camera*: Charles G. Clark. *Art*: Lyle R. Wheeler. *Editor*: Marjorie Fowler. *Music*: Cyril J. Mockridge. *Running time*: 90 minutes. De Luxe Color/Cinemascope.

CAST

Dan Dailey . . . . *Arthur Turner*
Ginger Rogers . . . . *Mildred Turner*
David Niven . . . . *Dr. Alan Coles*
Barbara Rush . . . . *Myra Hagerman*
Tony Randall . . . . *Cobbler*
Natalie Schafer . . . . *Mrs. Day*
Rachel Stephens . . . . *Miss Tacher*
John Wengraf . . . . *Dr. Krauss*
Cheryl Clarke . . . . *Melba*

STORY

In the mind-puffing world of fashionable Manhattan the psychiatrist is king. Dr. Alan Coles is a suave and polished example of the ilk, ministering to those with sick psyches but healthy bank balances.

His own reflexes suffer a severe jolt when Mildred, wife of film star Arthur Turner, pours out her latest stream of troubles, her husband's fixation for a wide-eyed wench named Myra Hagerman. Myra is the doctor's fiancée and they are on the verge of taking an ocean cruise and getting married on board.

Alan gets more shock treatment with the arrival of a highly eccentric patient, Cobbler, distraught over a lady, and it's Myra again.

In the emotional events that follow, Allan not only loses his fiancée but, shades of Freud, his own temper. Nevertheless, he patches up the marriage between Mildred and Arthur and leaves for his sea trip with a severe case of depression.

Myra doesn't turn up and Alan orders that his baggage be put ashore. And then Myra arrives, but only to make her last farewells. In doing so she is too late to leave the boat and hears the steward announce to Alan that his own luggage had been taken ashore.

This, interpreted as a chivalrous gesture, exercises a miraculous change in Myra's feelings. She indicates every readiness for a reconciliation.

In trouble with Dan Dailey.

With Barbara Rush.

NOTES

Feelings were very mixed about this film, as films about psychiatry tend to produce odd neuroses in audiences. The picture's combination of moments of reality with wild comedy and predictable send-ups of the head-shrinking business annoyed as many people as it charmed.

'Shrewd and wicked farce,' diagnosed the *Financial Times*. 'I haven't laughed so much for a long time,' confessed the *Sunday Despatch*.

'A dull consulting room comedy,' said *Time*. 'The ugliest sort of fun,' said the *Observer*.

Tony Randall, a young actor from Broadway, was duly discovered by everybody. 'A comedian of genius,' said critic Philip Oakes. But Hollywood negligently failed to exploit his full potential.

'Cinemascope here discovers a solution to the problem of filling its wide screen; the characters spend most of their time full length on the psychoanalyst's couch ... David Niven plays wittily as the consultant,' said the *Sunday Times*.

In a mixed and mixed-up reception Niven emerged liked by everybody. 'David Niven as the harassed consultant,' concluded the *Sunday Despatch*, 'has never been better.'

'David Niven, suave as ever...' *Daily Mail*. 'It is well acted, particularly by David Niven...' *Daily Mirror*. 'Admirably acted ....' *The Times*.

Niven as a shrink....

... a case of: Psychiatrist, sort thyself out.

MY MAN GODFREY

1957

Universal. *Producer*: Ross Hunter. *Director*: Henry Koster. *Script*: Everett Freeman, Peter Berneis, William Bowers—*based on a screenplay by* Morris Ryskind and Eric Hatch *from the novel by* Eric Hatch. *Camera*: William Daniels. *Art*: Alexander Golitzen, Richard H. Riedel. *Editor*: Milton Carruth. *Music*: Frank Skinner. *Running time*: 92 minutes. Technicolor/Cinemascope.

CAST

June Allyson . . . . *Irene*
David Niven . . . . *Godfrey*
Jessie Royce Landis . . . . *Angelica*
Robert Keith . . . . *Bullock*
Eva Gabor . . . . *Francesca*
Martha Hyer . . . . *Cordelia*
Jay Robinson . . . . *Vincent*
Jeff Donnell . . . . *Molly*
Herbert Anderson . . . . *Hubert*
Eric Sinclair . . . . *Brent*
Dabbs Greer . . . . *Lt. O'Connor*
Fred Essler . . . . *Captain*

STORY

Wild young socialite Irene Bullock picks up a waterfront tramp, takes him home and, although he roundly insults Irene's sister Cordelia, appoints him butler to the Bullock household.

He charms the whole brood of Bullocks, including Vincent, a broken-down pianist who has attached himself to the household. Only Cordelia holds out against his attractions and schemes to get him fired. Irene, however, falls steadily in love with him.

Confessing to the name of 'Godfrey', the stranger is officiating at one of the family's lavish charity parties when he meets a figure from his past in the shape of much married international play-girl, Francesca.

Far from being a genuine tramp Godfrey is actually an Austrian count impoverished during the war who took to sea as a deck-hand and jumped ship in New York.

Meantime odious Cordelia has hidden a bracelet under Godfrey's mattress as part of her campaign to get him sacked. The scheme misfires but Godfrey's past is out and his status as a legal resident comes under scrutiny.

He seals his popularity with the Bullocks, even winning over Cordelia, by helping Poppa Bullock escape bankruptcy, and then he gives himself up as an illegal immigrant. As a freighter ships him back to Europe lovelorn Irene arrives too late at the quayside and shouts a proposal of marriage across the water. He refuses on the grounds that he wouldn't want to be suspected of marrying her to gain citizenship.

She gets a lift on a pilot boat and intercepts the ship, and the captain agrees to marry the couple when they reach international waters.

NOTES

Another case of David Niven, admirably cast, in a remake of a venerated comedy of the thirties which starred William Powell and Carole Lombard. It is understandable, one supposes, to resent anybody messing about with a film we know and love, and quite regularly these sort of efforts get a frosty reception.

The man at the *New York Times* couldn't quite put his finger on why he didn't like the film and concluded his notice: 'Maybe June Allyson and David Niven are just not Miss Lombard and Mr. Powell.'

Universal labelled Niven and June Allyson 'zany society doll and a suave butler' but Niven weathered the storm.

The 'zany doll' stops her father (Robert Keith) paying off the butler. William Powell played the role in the 30s.

The mystery butler is recognised. David Niven among the ladies above stairs. . . .

. . . and below stairs.

Kine Weekly was more generous: 'David Niven has just the right approach as the wise, suave and good-looking Godfrey.'

After we get the original version out of our system we can often take a more objective view. I find the picture a great deal more entertaining than did the contemporary reviewers and I've seen them both and was wild about the original.

By 1968 the writer in *Movies On TV* described it as a disappointing re-make but added: 'Niven is fine but Miss Allyson is miscast and can't carry off the more subtle aspects of the script.'

Angela and Elkan Allan, writing in 1973 in *Movies On Television,* are much warmer. 'Competent remake . . . comes off extremely well, thanks to David Niven's cool and dry performance in the shoes of William Powell . . . June Allyson is OK as the girl . . . Henry Koster has wisely not tried to improve on the original . . .'

A characteristic Niven pose . . . attractive but not quite sure of himself.

BONJOUR TRISTESSE

1957

Wheel Productions. *Producer/director*: Otto Preminger. *Script*: Arthur Laurents—*from the novel by* Françoise Sagan. *Camera*: Georges Perinal. *Art*: Raymond Sims. *Editor*: Helga Cranston. *Music*: Georges Auric. *Running time*: 93 minutes. Technicolor and Black and White/Cinemascope.

CAST

Deborah Kerr. . . . . *Anne*
David Niven . . . . *Raymond*
Jean Seberg . . . . *Cecile*
Mylene Demongeot . . . . *Elsa*
Geoffrey Horne . . . . *Philippe*
Juliette Greco. . . . . *Night club singer*
Walter Chiari. . . . . *Pablo*
Martita Hunt . . . . *Philippe's mother*
Roland Culver . . . . *Mr. Lombard*
Jean Kent . . . . *Mrs. Lombard*
David Oxley . . . . *Jacques*
Elgar Andersen. . . . . *Denise*
Jeremy Burnham. . . . . *Hubert Duclos*
Eveline Eyfel . . . . *Maid*
Tutte Lemkow . . . . *Pierre Schube*

STORY

There is a warm, not to say slightly overheated, relationship between 17-year-old Cecile and her widowed father, Raymond. Raymond is a playboy around the most luxurious spots in France with a taste for a succession of young and nubile feminine playthings, a situation approved by his daughter in a most liberated manner.

They are holidaying amongst the South of France jet-set with daddy's latest showpiece, Elsa, in attendance. Then on the scene comes Anne Larsen, an older woman and a former flame of Raymond's, with plans to steer him into a more mature way of life. They become engaged. This doesn't suit Cecile, who sees a serious change in her special relationship with her father developing. She arranges with a boy-friend, Philippe, to pursue Elsa to make her father jealous. The scheme succeeds and Raymond is caught by Anne renewing his affair with Elsa.

Anne drives madly away from the scene and crashes into the sea. This leaves dad and daughter with a bleak future, conscious that their selfishness caused Anne's death.

Wealthy wastrels living it up on the French Riviera.

Playboy Niven, latest girl friend Mylene Demongeot and approving daughter Jean Seberg.

NOTES

Otto Preminger, having saved David Niven's career at a point when it was badly on the wane with a part in *The Moon is Blue,* engaged him again for this version of Françoise Sagan's trendy novel. Preminger generously spread Hollywood-style gloss all over the picture: scenery from the French Riviera, gowns by Givenchy, jewels by Cartier, accessories by Hermes but, unfortunately, little of the special qualities that made the Sagan story remarkable. That may not appear to be so sacriligious nowadays but the vacuous frivolity that was left does nothing to endear us to the film.

'Wealthy philanderers living a night-to-night existence among the fleshpots can become very tiresome on the screen,' sighed *The Times.* 'Even when they are invested with Mr. David Niven's apologetic charm.'

The *Daily Express* noted: 'David Niven was smooth and competent as the middle-aged, playboy father.'

'Long, untidy, muddled and mushy,' muttered the *Financial Times,* totally unimpressed by the show of wealth.

Otto Preminger Presents
DEBORAH KERR
DAVID NIVEN
JEAN SEBERG
MYLENE DEMONGEOT in
BONJOUR TRISTESSE
GEOFFREY HORNE
JULIETTE GRECO WALTER CHIARI

MARTITA HUNT ROLAND CULVER JEAN KENT DAVID OXLEY ELGA ANDERSEN SCREENPLAY BY ARTHUR LAURENTS BASED ON THE NOVEL BY FRANCOISE SAGAN MUSIC BY GEORGES AURIC PRODUCED AND DIRECTED BY OTTO PREMINGER CINEMASCOPE COLOR BY TECHNICOLOR RELEASED BY COLUMBIA PICTURES

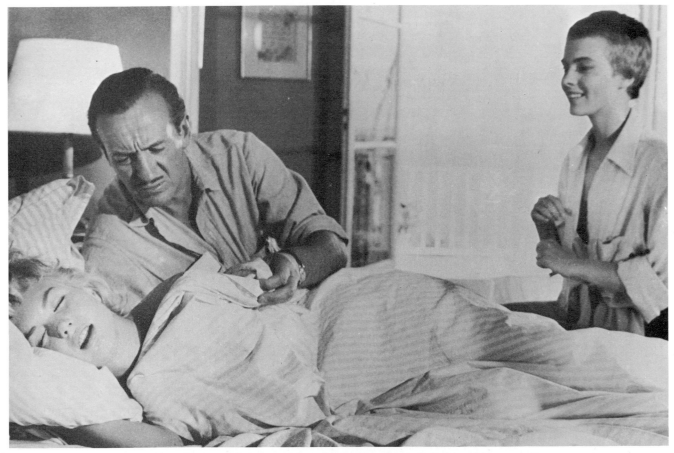

Otto Preminger made heavy-going of Francoise Sagan's fashionable novelette.

Otto Preminger, basically a rather agreeable, even kindly, man in private, adored giving realistic impressions of Himmler in public. Niven, who had got on well with him during *The Moon is Blue,* had a mighty clash with him on location in Paris: on this occasion Niven, as all present agreed, gave as good as he got.

It is doubtful if any one could have saved this film but David Niven came near to it, and Frank Jackson paid a very real tribute to his capabilities in *Reynold's News* when he wrote: 'Probably the only actor who could make the philanderer at all sympathetic.'

148

With Jean Seberg and Deborah Kerr, who tried to make an honest man of him.

SEPARATE TABLES

1958

A Clifton Productions Inc. Picture. *Producer*: Harold Hecht. *Director*: Delbert Mann. *Script*: Terence Rattigan, John Gay—*from the play by* Terence Rattigan. *Camera*: Charles Lang Jnr. *Music*: David Raskin. *Art*: Edward Carrere. *Editors*: Marjorie Fowler, Charles Ennis. *Miss Hayworth's gowns*: Edith Head. *Song 'Separate Tables' by* Harry Warren, Harold Adamson. *Running time*: 98 minutes.

CAST

Deborah Kerr . . . . *Sibyl Railton-Bell*
Rita Hayworth . . . . *Ann Shankland*
David Niven . . . . *Major Pollack*
Wendy Hiller . . . . *Miss Cooper*
Burt Lancaster . . . . *John Malcolm*
Gladys Cooper . . . . *Mrs. Railton-Bell*
Cathleen Nesbitt . . . . *Lady Matheson*
Felix Aylmer . . . . *Mr. Fowler*
Rod Taylor . . . . *Charles*
Audrey Dalton . . . . *Jean*
May Hallatt . . . . *Miss Meachum*
Priscilla Morgan . . . . *Doreen*
Hilda Plowright . . . . *Mabel*

STORY

The Beauregard Private Hotel at Bournemouth is the sort of place where some of the seedily genteel rejects of society huddle together in mutual insecurity. The prim but good-hearted Miss Cooper is the proprietress, and her mixed bag of boarders includes an American writer, John Malcolm, drowning the memory of something feminine and nasty in his past in drink, and hoping to marry his landlady.

Among the others are poor mouse Sibyl Railton-Bell, perpetually cowed by her crushing, sharp-tongued mother, and Major Pollack who combines a furtive air with a jaunty manner and regales other guests with tales of his days in action during the war.

Sibyl and the Major form a halting relationship of sorts but this is discouraged by Mrs. Railton-Bell in her best sarcastic manner.

She noses out a report in the local paper which reveals that the Major had been arrested for molesting women in a local cinema and, furthermore, which exposes his tales of high rank and daring deeds in the war as lies; he had never been higher than a lieutenant and sat out the conflict in an office in the R.A.S.C.

As Major Pollack (with Deborah Kerr), the portrait that won him an Oscar.

Deborah Kerr, in love with the bogus Major and over-shadowed by her tyranical mother (Gladys Cooper).

Two of the Major's fellow boarders, Rita Hayworth and Burt Lancaster.

Exposing him to the guests and her daughter, she demands that he be expelled from the hotel. In the meantime Miss Cooper has worries of her own. Film star Ann Shankland, John's former wife, arrives at the hotel to reclaim him. Deciding that it is she, after all, he really wants, Miss Cooper decides to bow out of their lives.

The Major and Sibyl, recovered from the shock of her mother's revelations, talk and find that, if nothing else, they have weaknesses in common.

He decides not to quit the hotel but to stay and face the guests. He appears at breakfast and, from their various separate tables, the guests murmur the conventional greetings. Mrs. Railton-Bell tries to get her daughter to leave the room but she turns to the Major's table and engages him in breakfast-time small talk. Her mother's power over her has at last been banished.

NOTES

This film, a major event in Niven's career for it won him his Oscar as best actor, was made by Burt Lancaster's film company—with partners Harold Hecht and James Hill—which produced a number of ambitious pictures with big star casts around this time, including *The Devil's Disciple*.

Terence Rattigan's original play was a double-bill in which the two major events at the hotel—the Sibyl–Major story and the John Malcolm–Miss Cooper story—formed the two plays with two players taking both sets of parts.

In the film the four parts were taken by four players and the tales intermingled. As a concession to United States audiences two of the characters were transformed into Americans.

The film was a triumph for David Niven: the *Daily Herald* headlined its notice 'Niven's Masterpiece' and critic Anthony Carthew wrote: 'I knew I was seeing a piece of acting worth an Oscar—or, what is more valuable, the gratitude of the millions of people who will see this fine film.

'Niven has shed his Martini manner and his continued gaiety. In its place he puts a thoughtful study of a sad, lonely genuine human being.'

He ended: 'At the age of 48, he joins the select ranks of the screen masters.'

The man Hollywood had written off only five years before heard his praises sung loud and clear. 'Astoundingly real, true, touching'—*The People*; 'Niven is excellent'—*Time*; 'David Niven crowns his considerably successful career with a shining performance'—*Evening News*; 'Mr. Niven ... gives the exact feel of an ingrowing shabbiness pressing on the quick of a frightened soul'—*Observer*; 'David Niven acts out the finest role of his career'—*Daily Sketch*; 'David Niven's Major with his loping military gait, the timing of his peppery officer's jargon, and the bland, faintly shadowed star of a man whose life is a lie, is beautifully characterised'—*Sunday Times*.

The Times paid tribute to Deborah Kerr's contribution while expressing doubts about the film's treatment of its subject. 'Mr. Niven and Miss Kerr, giving inarticulate accounts of their own forms of loneliness and fear in a world that is too much for them, transcend the entertaining superficialities which are the common coin of *Separate Tables* as a whole.'

There were few dissenting voices. Among this minority the *Financial Times* reviewer remarked: 'Scarcely any of the characters in *Separate Tables* seem even on nodding terms with life' and says later, 'David Niven as the Major appears to be more concerned with polishing a series of mannerisms and tricks of speech than with getting beneath the sensitive skin of his part.' One would hardly have expected the actor to have got beneath the sensitive skin of a character hardly on nodding terms with life.

The award of the Oscar to Niven aroused the wrath of Andrew Sarris, film critic of *The Village Voice,* also Associate Professor of Cinema at Columbia University. He seemed annoyed because James Stewart didn't get the Oscar instead.

He wrote in an essay printed in his book *The Primal Screen*: 'This was an era in which feeble talents like Ernest Borgnine and David Niven were winning Oscars for characterisations that proclaimed their own drabness.'

An odd way to champion James Stewart, but then you don't make your name as a trendy and cheeky reviewer by following the common critical herd praising David Niven and enjoying *Marty*.

The New York film critics (fifteen from the metropolitan newspapers) gave their votes for 1958 to *The Defiant Ones* over *Separate Tables,* but David Niven was their choice as best actor with Alec Guinness a close second.

With Wendy Hiller.

ASK ANY GIRL

1959

Euterpe Productions. *Producer*: Joe Pasternak. *Director*: Charles Walters. *Script*: George Wells—*from the novel by* Winifred Wolfe. *Camera*: Robert Bronner. *Editor*: John McSweeney Jnr. *Art*: William A. Horning, Urie McCleary. *Costumes*: Helen Rose. *Music*: Jeff Alexander. *Running time*: 101 minutes. Metrocolor/Cinemascope.

CAST

David Niven . . . . *Miles Doughton*
Shirley MacLaine . . . . *Meg Wheeler*
Gig Young . . . . *Evan Doughton*
Rod Taylor . . . . *Ross Taford*
Jim Backus . . . . *Mr. Maxwell*
Claire Kelly . . . . *Lisa*
Elisabeth Fraser . . . . *Jeannie Boyden*
Dody Heath. . . . . *Terri Richards*
Read Morgan . . . . *Bert*
Carmen Philips . . . . *Refined young lady*

STORY

Kooky Meg Wheeler arrives in New York straight from back of the beyond to hack a career for herself out of the asphalt jungle. Losing her luggage at the station she finds refuge in a hotel for women (no kissing permitted beyond the lobby, no men allowed beyond the first floor) sharing with three girls; Lisa, Jeanne and Terri.

She gets a job as a receptionist at a sweater factory—Kampus Knits—and a date with Ross Taford, a knave with the girls. He takes her out to his Connecticut home to meet the family—when the family are away. Shocked by his intentions Meg cancels the romance.

Back at the office the boss, Mr. Maxwell, makes a lecherous move. She quits the job.

She is then hired as a field research worker at an ad. agency. Miles Doughton, the slightly prissy head man, rejects her but brother Evan (another wolf) takes her on in all ways. This is real love for Meg but to

Gig Young is the wolf, Niven the stuffy one, but soon awakened by Shirley MacLaine.

Part of the awakening process.

Familiar Niven look for the publicity photographers.

After his Oscar, it's back to the sort of film where you pose for this sort of promotion still with ... What did they call it? Plenty of cheesecake.

Evan she's just another in the harem. Softening, Miles tries to help. He contacts the Evan girl pack and, using company skills on motivational research, relays to Meg the sort of composite cutie she must become to secure Evan one hundred per cent.

This works and Evan proposes but by now Meg, eyes opened, realises it's Miles she really wants.

NOTES

This turned out to be one of Joe Pasternark's fun films with that extra quality, and a great vehicle for Hollywood's latest novelty, Shirley MacLaine. She won the Silver Bear as the 'best foreign actress' at the 1959 Berlin Film Festival and the B.F.A. award in the same category.

But it was a palpable hit for David Niven, too. 'Mr. Niven has certainly taken on a new lease of life since about four films ago,' said the *Daily Mail*. 'This latest

Off-set still with Mickey Shaughnessy (who guested in the film), Shirley MacLaine and director Charles Walters and producer Joe Pasternak on either side.

With Shirley MacLaine and Gig Young.

effort seems to confirm him as a captain and *chef du protocol* of Hollywood's British colony for the next 20 years or so.'

The reviews, all in all, sounded the sort of paean of praise that must be music to any actor's ears.

'David Niven, all polish and impeccable timing, makes every gesture tell...'—*Sunday Times*.

'Niven's easy, polished performance is splendid...'—*Evening News*.

'The quiet skill of David Niven and Shirley MacLaine...'—*Time and Tide*. 'Mr. Niven partners her perfectly...'—*News Chronicle*.

'The poker-faced playing of Mr. Niven set in deliberate contrast to the natural exuberance of Miss MacLaine ...'—*The Times*.

'The combined talents of David Niven and Shirley MacLaine make it a friendly, easy show...'—*The Observer*.

'Acted with gusto by Niven and Young and happily full of Shirley MacLaine...'—*Daily Express*.

This was not, happily, David Niven doing another undervalued salvage job. The film itself got an all-round warm welcome. 'Jolly,' said the New Yorker; 'An hilarious film,' said the *Daily Express*.

A pity though that Niven, with his sole Oscar behind him for a good but uncharacteristic performance, should still lack a major prize for the sort of work he does supremely well.

This Niven–MacLaine twosome was part of a stills session cooked-up by M.G.M.'s publicity department and called The Seven Lively Arts of Making a Man Say 'Yes'.

HAPPY ANNIVERSARY

1959

With Mitzi Gaynor.

Fields Production Inc. *Producer*: Ralph Fields. *Director*: David Miller. *Script*: Joseph Fields, Jerome Chodorov—*based on their play*, Anniversary Waltz. *Camera*: Lee Garmes. *Music*: Sol Kapla, Robert Allen. *Editor*: Richard Meyer. *Design*: Paul Heller. *Running time*: 83 minutes.

CAST

David Niven . . . . *Chris Walters*
Mitzi Gaynor . . . . *Alice Walters*
Carl Reiner . . . . *Bud*
Loring Smith . . . . *Mr. Gans*
Monique Van Vooren . . . . *Jeanette*
Phyllis Povah . . . . *Mrs. Gans*
Patty Duke . . . . *Debbie*
Elizabeth Wilson . . . . *Millie*
Kevin Coughlin . . . . *Okkie*

STORY

With a whole lot of ill luck awaiting them Chris and Alice Walters are busy celebrating their 13th wedding anniversary. Under the influence of the convivial champagne at the anniversary dinner Chris is rash enough to confide to Alice's shocked parents that they had actually been consummating the marriage a year before the lawful date in a handy hotel.

This tit-bit of information is overheard by the Walters's children, Okkie and the diabolical Debbie.

Alice is wild with Chris for his indiscretions, and her fury is not abated when they see on television daughter Debbie making a frank confession of her parent's infidelity at a youth forum.

At the height of the storm Chris stamps out. He returns later, contrite, but only to hear from Alice

With Mitzi Gaynor . . . not the happiest of partnerships.

that she is leaving him. The foundering marriage is only saved by a providential telephone call to announce that Alice's pregnancy test had proved she was to have another baby. In view of the quality of the existing Walters's kids that might seem a mixed blessing.

NOTES

The swinging sixties not yet mobile, United Artists, who were releasing this picture, got last minute cold feet at some of the moral implications.

They asked Niven to dub an extra line of dialogue into the picture saying: 'I was wrong. I should never have taken Alice to that hotel room before we were married.'

Niven refused indignantly. 'It made me sound as if I had made a dirty picture,' he said. Another actor had to imitate Niven's voice and do the job.

It was very much a storm in a cup of tepid tea. 'The plot is a house of comic greeting cards . . .' said *Time*. We didn't like it any better; in fact, rather worse. 'David Niven is an accomplished comedian but not any of his skills can do much for *Happy Anniversary*,' said *Time and Tide*.

Once again Hollywood's cautionary attitudes had turned a witty, mildly shocking satirical stage play, knocking a whole host of American institutions from television to frightful Yankee kids, into inevitable leaden compromise.

'David Niven has been choosing himself such good parts lately that I am surprised that he should consent to do *Happy Anniversary*,' said the *Daily Mail* sadly. 'One wonders how players as charming as David Niven and Mitzi Gaynor ever came to be mixed up with it,' said the *Daily Telegraph*.

But 'The lines are often funny . . .' admitted the *Financial Times,* and *The Times* found 'Mr. Niven flourishing his particular brand of incisive suavity.'

159

As a husband and wife team, David Niven and the mercurial Mitzi Gaynor in a naughty domestic comedy that wasn't naughty enough.

With Carl Reiner, Monique Van Vooren and Mitzi Gaynor.

PLEASE DON'T EAT THE DAISIES

1960

Euterpe Production. *Producer*: Joe Pasternak. *Associate Producer*: Martin Melcher. *Director*: Charles Walters. *Script*: Isobel Lennart—*from the novel by* Jean Kerr. *Camera*: Robert Bronner. *Art*: George W. Davies, Hans Peters. *Music*: David Rose. *Editor*: John McSweeney. *Costumes*: Morton Haack. *Running time*: 111 minutes. Metrocolor/Cinemascope.

CAST

Doris Day . . . . *Kate Mackay*
David Niven . . . . *Lawrence Mackay*
Janis Paige . . . . *Deborah Vaughn*
Spring Byington . . . . *Mrs. Suzie Robinson*
Richard Haydn . . . . *Alfred North*
Patsy Kelly . . . . *Maggie*
Jack Weston . . . . *Joe Positano*
John Harding . . . . *Rev. Dr. McQuarry*
Margaret Lindsay . . . . *Mona James*
Carmen Phillips . . . . *Mary Smith*
Mary Patton . . . . *Mrs. Hunter*
Charles Herbert . . . . *David Mackay*
Stanley Livingston . . . . . . *Gabriel Mackay*
Flip Mark . . . . *George Mackay*
Baby Gellert . . . . *Adam Mackay*

STORY

From the comfortable scholarship of Columbia University Professor Lawrence Mackay leaves to join the bloodbath that passes for dramatic criticism when practised in New York by the famous (or infamous) 'butchers of Broadway'.

His very first stint of reviewing produces his first crisis of conscience. The play is produced by old friend Alfred North and critic Mackay considers it a stinker. Should he slaughter the play as principle demands and ruin his friendship? He compromises by attacking the play but praises the producer's past successes.

Like most compromises this one doesn't work. North is furious and the new critic is slapped by the outraged star of the show Deborah Vaughn in Sardi's, New York's show-biz eating house.

His consequent fame arising from the scandal rather goes to his academic head and this is not very popular with wife Kate. The family, with four sons, moves into a new country home but domesticity, after a blissful ten-year run, is heading for a flop.

Kate joins the local amateur dramatic group and North suggests the company's play should be a slice of dramatic fustian written long ago by husband Lawrence.

Domestic bliss with Doris Day.

As a drama critic, off duty, off set with Doris Day. The real-life film critics waded into this one.

Lawrence, hearing of this malicious venture, is furious. But the play—re-written as a comedy—is a great hit and a mollified and humbled drama critic is restored to a life of marital contentment.

NOTES

Being a film from the stable of the twinkle-eyed Joe Pasternak—whose main object in life seemed to be to provide undemanding entertainment for an audience of simpletons—this was no subtle send-up of the world of the all-powerful New York drama critics. A pity, because peeping through Niven's hamstrung performance are tantalising glimpses of the sort of job he could have done with the part if only someone in charge of the venture could have been inspired by the sort of thinking that created the George Sanders role in *All About Eve*.

It was not much of a feast to set before the critics and so their almost unanimous disapproval can't be attributed to ruffled *amour-propre*.

'It would do my ego no end of good if I felt that British critics wielded as much power as Niven the critic does,' said Margaret Hinxman with good humour in the *Daily Herald*.

'I have never seen David Niven and Doris Day so poorly served,' said the *Daily Telegraph*.

Never mind, David Niven had something much better coming up just around the corner.

Costume designer Morton Haack and Janis Paige with Niven between shots.

It looks like a rehearsal for his later part as Dracula in *Vampira* but the expression actually provoked by the approach of actress Janis Paige.

With Doris Day, Spring Byington.

THE GUNS OF NAVARONE

1961

Open Road Films. *Producers*: Carl Foreman, Cecil Ford. *Director*: J. Lee Thompson. *Script*: Carl Foreman—*from the novel by* Alistair MacLean. *Associate Producer*: Leon Becker. *Music*: Dimitri Tiomkin. *Camera*: Oswald Morris. *Designer*: Geoffrey Drake. *Editor*: Alan Orbiston. *Special Effects*: Bill Warrington, Wally Veevers. *Sound Editor*: Vivian C. Greenham. *Assistant Director*: Peter Yates. *Running time*: 157 minutes. Technicolor/Cinemascope.

CAST

Gregory Peck . . . . *Captain Mallory*
David Niven . . . . *Corporal Miller*
Anthony Quinn. . . . . . . *Colonel Andrea Stavros*
Stanley Baker. . . . . *C.P.O. Brown*
Anthony Quayle . . . . . . *Major Franklin*
James Darren. . . . . *Private Pappadimos*
Irene Papas . . . . *Maria*
Gia Scala . . . . *Anna*
James Robertson Justic . . *Jensen*

Richard Harris . . . . *Barnsby*
Bryan Forbes . . . . *Cohn*
Allan Cuthbertson . . . . . *Baker*
Michael Trubshawe . . . . *Weaver*
Percy Herbert. . . . . *Grogan*
Albert Lieven . . . . *Commandant*
Norman Wooland . . . . . *Group Captain*

STORY

The Germans have occupied and fortified the tiny Greek island of Navarone off the coast of Turkey. They have mounted, in impregnable positions, the most powerful guns in the world. It is 1943 and these guns now menace a vital Allied operation, with many British ships and lives at stake.

Allied intelligence plan a desperate attempt to destroy the guns by means of a small group of saboteurs. The group will scale the island's south cliff, so sheer that the Germans leave it unguarded, penetrate the fortress housing the guns, and blow them up.

High adventure again. With Gregory Peck and Anthony Quinn.

In the enemy camp, David Niven with Gia Scala and James Darren.

Major 'Lucky' Franklin, who conceived the idea, is the leader. He picks for his team Captain Mallory, once a world famous mountaineer, fluent in German and French; Colonel Andrea Stavros, of the Greek Army; Corporal Miller, high explosives expert; C.P.O. Telegraphist Brown, the handiest man with a knife in the Middle East; and Private Pappadimos, a baby-faced killer.

On Navarone the men make contact with two women partisans, one of whom, just to add to their burdens, turns out to be a traitor. Major Franklin is injured early in the operation and it is left to Captain Mallory to lead the band through to the triumphant conclusion of its mission.

NOTES

This was a mammoth and spectacular production by independent producer Carl Foreman, an American operating in London, which went all-out to beat every other mammoth and spectacular film ever shot. It took two years to make and devoured—and earned—vast sums of money. It was said that the publicity machine alone cost as much as the entire budget for Foreman's earlier and more modest success *The Mouse That Roared*.

The publicity rivalled the drum-beating efforts of *Around The World in Eighty Days*, and the *Daily Express*, announcing the project, said, agog with excitement, 'Talks are going on to cast five of the world's top stars for it—William Holden, Marlon Brando, Alec Guinness, Cary Grant and Jack Hawkins.'

The Express proved to be as ill-informed as it was over-excited. The star cast turned out to be Gregory Peck, David Niven, Anthony Quinn, Stanley Baker and Anthony Quayle.

The finished picture lived up to its publicity barrage. 'The film is absolutely superlative of its sort,' said the *Sunday Telegraph*, 'right up to the very end when we are treated to what must be the most ear-shattering bang in the whole history of the sound film.'

What with the super-decibel sound track, the scintillating special effects and the nerve-jangling suspense cunningly maintained by director J. Lee Thompson, there was little scope left for refinement of acting; no one would pretend the characters or their dialogue were much more than superior comic strip.

But, said the *Evening News*, 'Gregory Peck, David Niven and Anthony Quinn give brilliant performances.'

However the *Guardian* noted sympathetically: 'David Niven, as the gentlemanly other ranker, has an impossible course to steer.'

The Times saw David Niven 'as the standard type of laconic and carefree Englishman, a gentleman

Sent to destroy the guns of Navarone. James Darren, Stanley Baker, David Niven, Gregory Peck, Anthony Quinn and Anthony Quayle.

In action with Gregory Peck.

ranker who quickly loses patience with this particular spree.'

David Niven as a mere corporal had nose-dived in rank. This irritated the lady from the *Observer*.

'Like all male British stars David Niven has an inescapable military rank,' she wrote,' and his is not a pip less than second lieutenant.

'The excuse that he refused a commission because he wanted to avoid the responsibility for killing people is scarcely acceptable when the character has such lip-clenching and absolutely officer-like lines of determination around the jaw.'

But David Niven may have been shrewder in taking the part than people imagined at the time. It's not many actors can compete with the most explosive moment in cinema history and still emerge as a subject of controversy.

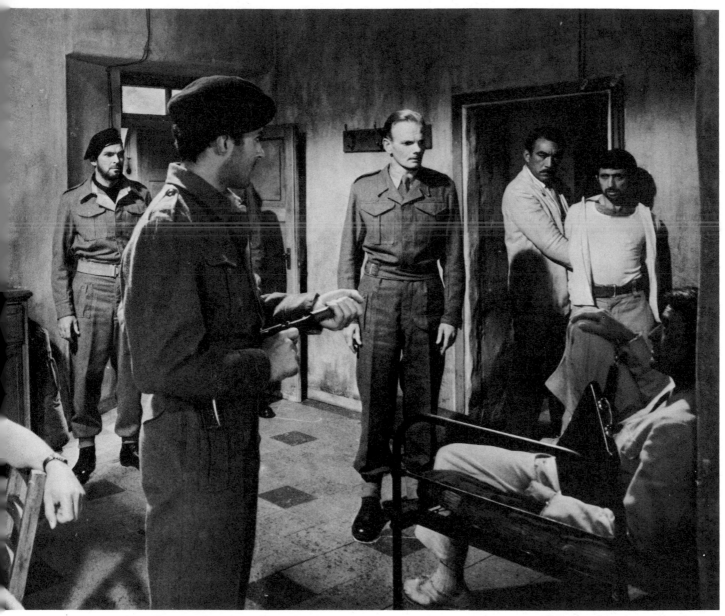

Niven may have been reduced to the rank of corporal for this one but he still sets all an example of how to remain calm in a crisis.

Relaxing, in a manner of speaking, before the biggest bang in cinema history.

THE BEST OF ENEMIES

(Italian title: I DUE NEMICI)

1961

Dino De Laurentiis Production. *Producer*: Dino De Laurentiis. *Director*: Guy Hamilton. *Script*: Jack Pulman—*from a story by* Luciano Vincenzoni. *Camera*: Guiseppe Rotunno. *Music*: Nino Rota. *Art*: Mario Garbuglia. *Editor*: Burt Bates. *Costumes*: Ezio Frigerio. *Running time*: 104 minutes. Technicolor/Technirama.

CAST

David Niven . . . . *Major Richardson*
Alberto Sordi . . . . *Captain Blasi*
Michael Wilding . . . . . . *Lieutenant Burke*
Amedeo Nazzari . . . . *Major Fornari*
Harry Andrews . . . . *Captain Rootes*
David Opatoshu . . . . . . *Captain Bernasconi*
Aldo Giuffre . . . . *Sergeant Todini*
Tiberio Mitri . . . . *Moccaia*
Kenneth Fortescue . . . . . *Lieutenant Thomlinson*
Duncan Macrae . . . . *Sergeant Trevethan*
Noel Harrison . . . . *Lieutenant Hillary*
Robert Desmond . . . . . . *Private Slinger*
Bernard Cribbens . . . . . . *Tanner*
Ronald Fraser . . . . *Prefect*
Pietro Marescalchi . . . . . *Corporal Bortolin*
Allesandro Ninchi . . . . . . *Lieutenant Del Pra*

STORY

Major Richardson, a very pukka British officer operating against the Italians in a desert warfare in Ethiopia in 1941, is captured by an enemy patrol commanded by Captain Blasi. Blasi, however, releases him on the tacit understanding that his group will be allowed to reach a nearby Italian-held fort without interference from British troops.

When the Major returns to base his superior refuses to carry out any such undertaking and orders Major Richardson out to the attack.

The Italians, called upon to surrender, scuttle out of the back of the fort with Major Richardson and his men in pursuit.

A forest fire drives both groups to the safety of a river. The British take the Italians prisoners. Both have lost their rations and much equipment and, harassed by tribesmen, decide to join forces on a strictly temporary basis: when the situation is secure the Italians must revert to prisoner status.

But when civilisation is regained it turns out to be Italian-held territory and the roles are reversed. The arrival of a British rescue force establishes the Italians as prisoners once again.

Back at base Captain Blasi and his men await transportation to a P.O.W. camp as Major Richardson and his troops march past. Major Richardson orders his men to present arms in salutation.

NOTES

We reach the era of multi-national film production, and in *The Best of Enemies* British and Italian actors and technicians joined forces (with David Niven also representing a box-office attraction for America) and British, Italian—and a dash of American—money backed the project.

It was a highly successful debut for Niven in this sort of enterprise. In a picture which satirised the attitudes of the British and Italian military Niven was required not only to guy the sort of officer he had played so many times before in the cinema but also the Sandhurst-trained British officer he had been in real life before turning to acting as a career. He did it impeccably.

A film sending up war could hardly appeal to the bellicose *Daily Express* and its critic Leonard Mosley (himself a war chronicler of the traditional type) said: 'I split my sides with boredom . . . Niven is a British officer with the heart of a lion but not a brain in his head.'

At the other extreme the *Daily Worker* disapproved

of it, too. 'Under the disguise of anti-war comedy, its aim is to obscure the true character of fascism,' scolded its critic.

On a more relevant level the *Sunday Times* summed up the film's achievements. 'The joke turns out to lie in contrasts of character intensified by the circumstances of war: the playing-field attitude of the Englishman leads him into the same absurd situations as the unmilitary mood of the Italians.'

The *Sunday Times* critic, in company with many others, loudly praised the performance of Italy's Alberto Sordi ('the jewel of the piece') but concluded: 'One should never underestimate David Niven. He is still one of the most durable of polished comedians.'

The *Daily Herald* said: 'David Niven . . . and Alberto Sordi . . . delicately walk a tightrope between the slapstick and the serious.'

'Niven gives a typically stylish performance,' said the *Observer*. 'David Niven, excellent as usual,' said the *News of the World*.

'Sandhurst-trained David Niven never lets down the light comedy side of officership,' noted *Time*.

THE CAPTIVE CITY

(Italian title: LE CITTA PRIGIONIERA)

(U.S. title: THE CONQUERED CITY)

1962

Maxima Film for Lux Film—Maxima Film—Galatea S.p.A. *Director*: Joseph Anthony. *Script*: Guy Elmes, Marc Brandel, Eric Bergovici—*from the book* The Captive City *by* John Appleby. *Camera*: Leonida Barboni. *Sets*: Mario Chiari. *Costumes*: Maria de Matteis. *Editor*: Mario Bonotti. *Special effects*: Stacchini. *Music*: Piero Piccioni. *Running time*: 108 minutes.

CAST

David Niven . . . . *Peter Whitefield*
Ben Gazzara . . . . *George Stubbs*
Michael Craig . . . . *Captain Robert Elliot*
Martin Balsam . . . . *Joseph Feinberg*
Lea Massari . . . . *Lelia Mendoris*
Clelia Matania . . . . *Climedes*
Giulio Bosetti . . . . *Narriman*
Percy Herbert . . . . *Sergeant Reed*
Ivo Garrani . . . . *Mavroti*
Odoardo Spadara . . . . . . *Janny Mendoris*
Roberto Risso . . . . *Loveday*
Venantino Venantini . . . . . *General Foroulan*
Carlo Hintermann . . . . . . *Tank's sergeant*
Adelmo Fraia . . . . *Antrea*
also starring
Daniela Rocca . . . . *as Doushka*

STORY

The British have liberated Athens as World War II ends but are in turn attacked by certain Greek army and partisan groups under General Foroulan. Peter Whitefield, an officer in the Balkan Information Service with the emergency rank of major, is trapped in the Hotel Zeus with a small group including Mendoris, the hotel's owner, his daughter Lelia, a beautiful Greek girl, Doushka, and an American captain, George Stubbs.

Whitefield is joined by Captain Elliot when a British rescue attempt fails. He gets orders to hold on at any cost, puzzling how to do this until he discovers the cellar is stuffed with arms and ammunition sorely needed by the partisans.

His defence is hampered by the knowledge that among

his party is an enemy agent. In the end he manages
to destroy both the agent and the weapons and escape
to safety with Lelia.

NOTES
This was a routine gallop for Officer Niven over a
conventional battle course. The results didn't seem
to please anyone much and the film was slipped out
without ceremony.
'Tedious melodrama,' said the *BFI Bulletin*, 'David
Niven and Michael Craig make the best of their
lines...'
'David Niven gives his usual suave but resolute performance as Whitefield,' said Margaret Hinxman in
The Daily Cinema.

GUNS OF DARKNESS

1962

Cavalcade—Concorde. *Producers*: Ben Kadish, Thomas Clyde. *Director*: Anthony Asquith. *Script*: John Mortimer *from novel* Act of Mercy *by* Francis Clifford. *Camera*: Robert Krasker. *Art*: John Howell. *Editor*: Frederick Wilson. *Wardrobe*: Anthony Mendleson. *Music*: Benjamin Frankel. *Running time*: 102 minutes.

CAST

Leslie Caron . . . . *Claire Jordan*
David Niven . . . . *Tom Jordan*
James Robertson Justice . . . . . *Hugo Bryant*
David Opatoshu . . . . *Rivera*
Richard Pearson . . . . *Bastian*
Eleanor Summerfield . . . . *Mrs. Bastian*
Derek Godfrey . . . . *Hernandez*
Ian Hunter . . . . *Dr. Swann*
Sandor Eles . . . . *Lieutenant Gomez*

STORY

As the British residents of Tribulacion, capital city of a South American republic, see in the New Year, a revolutionary coup led by army chief Zoreno sees out the old, and liberal, regime of President Rivera.

Tom Jordan, employed by Napier International Plantations, is a man with his own private turbulence; he is bored and contemptuous of his life and surroundings, embattled with his wife, Claire, who is planning to leave him, and at loggerheads with his boss, Hugo Bryant.

The realities of the other world are brought home to him when he finds the badly wounded ex-president dumped in his car. He decides upon an act of mercy

Just one of the ordeals when Niven and Leslie Caron (as his wife) get mixed up with a South American revolution.

Seeing in the New Year with James Robertson Justice and Leslie Caron.

and resolves to drive Rivera to the safety of the border. His wife, now revealed as pregnant, accompanies him on the mission.

Zoreno's men, aware of what's happening, are on their track. After a hazardous journey the trio are within sight of the border when they are captured.

Tom, who earlier had been horrified at the casual way Rivera had wished to kill a child who had recognised him, finds he must kill the officer in charge of their captors if they are to break free.

He does so and they escape to safety over the border. Tom's boss has a confession for Tom to sign that will exonerate the company. He refuses.

NOTES

Anthony Asquith injected his own hatred of violence into this film. Much of the time it's conventional escape—though not entirely escapist—stuff, combining some interesting observations on the nature of conscience and guilt. The blending of *Boy's Own* story and thinking man's philosophy never quite worked. Perhaps the gentle Anthony Asquith lacked the necessary savage touch to bring it off.

David Niven worked hard on his far from conventional hero character.

'The planter is such a convincing figure, a man in agony because he sees and asks too much, that you never think of him as David Niven until the film ends,' said the *Daily Mail*.

'Mr. Niven, as always, manages to give the edge of individuality a flippant manner,' said *The Times*.

The *Financial Times* noted the hero as 'An immature, disillusioned, rebellious Englishman (played by David Niven, who seems continually to improve as an actor).'

The *Daily Telegraph*, finding the film dramatically weak, remarked: 'No blame for dissatisfaction on David Niven whose Jordan needs more writing than better acting.'

There weren't many cheerful moments for David Niven in *Guns of Darkness* but here's one of them.

With James Robertson Justice.

55 DAYS IN PEKING

1963

Samuel Bronston Production. *Producer*: Samuel Bronston. *Executive Associate Producer*: Michael Waszynski. *Director*: Nicholas Ray. *Script*: Philip Yordan, Bernard Gordon—*with additional dialogue by* Rober Hamer. *Art*: Veniero Colasanti, John Moore. *Music*: Dimitri Tiomkin. *Camera*: Jack Hildyard. *Second Unit Directors*: Andrew Marton, Noel Howard. *Special Effects*: Alex Weldon. *Running time*: 154 minutes. Technicolor/Super Technirama.

CAST

Charlton Heston . . . . . *Major Matt Lewis*
David Niven . . . . *Sir Arthur Robertson*
Ava Gardner . . . . *Baroness Natalie Ivanoff*
Robert Helpmann . . . . *Prince Tuan*
Flora Robson . . . . *Dowager Empress Tzu Hsi*
Leo Genn . . . . *General Jung-Lu*
John Ireland . . . . *Sergeant Harry*
Kurt Kasznar. . . . . . . *Baron Sergei Ivanoff*
Paul Lukas . . . . *Dr. Steinfeldt*
Harry Andrews . . . . . *Father de Bearn*
Elizabeth Sellars . . . . . *Lady Sarah Robertson*
Lynne Sue Moon . . . . *Teresa*
Jerome Thor . . . . *Lt. Andy Marshall*
Jacques Sernas . . . . . *Major Bobrinski*
Alfred Lynch . . . . *Gerald*
Ichizo Itami. . . . . *Colonel Shiba*
Joseph Furst . . . . *Captain Hanselman*

STORY

In the spring of 1900 the Dowager Empress of China declares war on the foreign devils infesting the land and the Boxer rebellion is born. The rebels attack Legation City in Peking, the home of eleven foreign embassies.

The people of the different nations unite in defence and the siege of the compound begins officially at 5 pm June 20.

Sir Arthur Robertson, the British envoy, is responsible for swaying fearful hearts and inspiring resistance. Major Matt Lewis, Lieutenant Andy Marshall and Sergeant Marshall are on hand with a detachment of American marines.

After the first five days of fighting the defenders get the bad news that expected reinforcements have been cut off. Lieutenant Marshall is killed and it becomes Matt Lewis's task to break the news to his 12-year-old daughter Teresa, whose Chinese mother died soon after she was born. Matt undertakes to care for her.

He has involvements, also, with an older lady, Natalie, a notorious Russian baroness who nurses the wounded.

As the situation deteriorates the Empress demands that the defenders surrender. Sir Arthur thinks a little offensive action would be the best reply. With Matt and Colonel Shiba, a Japanese, they burrow through the sewers and blow up the Chinese arsenal.

With food running out, Natalie trades her jewels for food and medicine but is hit by a sniper while getting the supplies into the compound.

Boxers close in for the final assault using a primitive form of rocket launcher to set the place on fire. The defenders devise an equally primitive form of napalm (kerosene in bottles propelled by catapult) to destroy the attack.

Natalie dies of her wound. Rescuers arrive. Sir Arthur and his lady plan their return to Britain and restless Matt rides away with Teresa into a sunset of yellow Chinese dust.

NOTES

Samuel Bronston, who employed David Niven in this film, appeared to represent the last fling of old-style Hollywood, except that his H.Q. was Madrid and not California.

He first attracted world-wide attention with his spectacular (though not particularly successful) re-make

Charlton Heston, Ava Gardner and Niven in full diplomatic garb.

of *King of Kings,* followed it with an undoubted hit, *El Cid,* and then turned his hand to this curious version of the siege of the embassies during the Boxer rebellion.

A small, delicately-made man, impeccably turned out right down to his carefully manicured hands, he looked as exquisitely finished as the most precious of his costly props. Seeming to hold power in Spain second only to Franco he also had the gift for raising huge sums to meet his colossal budgets: *55 Days in Peking* was said to have cost £4 million and certainly looks it.

The crash was bound to come and it did, but for a brief spell Samuel Bronston re-created a lost luscious, extravagant era.

The story was cunningly devised to provide the special effects department with the star part and what gaps they left the scenic and costume people carefully papered over.

David Niven described it as 'An open-air Western in Chinese.' The *Daily Express* called it: 'Spectacle on the grand scale.'

'What Nicholas Ray has made of it,' said the *New Statesman,* 'is a series of magnificent occasions.'

In a film like this the acting honours tend to fall on the strenuously over-worked extras.

'Pictorially this is a beautiful film,' said the *Sunday Times.* 'The characters, with the possible exception of the American major ... are conventional siege figures.'

Time took the mickey: 'The demoralised diplomats are all for pulling out when the fireworks begin, but Ambassador Niven—gnawing his moustache to denote deep thought—counsels them to stay put...'

But elsewhere, peering through the smoke of battle, critics found once again that David Niven could be relied upon to put on a performance whatever the opposition.

'Once the big guns come into action there is little room for acting ... Mr. Niven plays with his habitual authority...' said *The Times.*

'Of a large and largely expendable star cast, only David Niven manages to transcend the absurdity of his lordly role with practical authority,' wrote the *Monthly Film Bulletin* of the British Film Institute.

Fighting the Boxer rebellion in Madrid: Charlton Heston, Ava Gardner and David Niven.

A moment of peaceful conversation between the burst of special effects with Charlton Heston.

There was said to have been a world-wide shortage of Chinese waiters during the filming of *55 Days of Peking*. They were all working on the film as extras.

184

THE PINK PANTHER

1964

A Blake Edwards Production for The Mirisch Company. *Producer*: Martin Jurow. *Director*: Blake Edwards. *Script*: Maurice Richlin, Blake Edwards. *Camera*: Philip Lathrop. *Music*: Henry Mancini. *Art*: Fernando Carrere. *Editor*: Ralph Winters. *Special Effects*: Lee Zavitz. *Choreography*: Hermes Pan. *Special Costume Design*: Yves St. Laurent. *Wardrobe*: Dario Cecchi. *Running time*: 114 minutes. Technicolor/Technirama.

CAST

David Niven . . . . *Sir Charles Lytton*
Peter Sellers . . . . *Inspector Jacques Clouseau*
Robert Wagner . . . . . . *George*
Capucine . . . . *Simone Clouseau*
Claudia Cardinale . . . . *Princess Dala*
Brenda de Banzie . . . . *Angela Dunning*
Fran Jeffries . . . . *Greek 'cousin'*
Colin Gordon . . . . *Tucker*
John le Mesurier . . . . . *Defence attorney*
James Lanphier . . . . . *Saloud*
Guy Thomajan . . . . . . *Artoff*
Michael Trubshawe . . . *The novelist*
Riccardo Billi . . . . *Greek shipowner*
Meri Wells . . . . *Hollywood starlet*
Martin Miller . . . . *Photographer*

STORY

Sir Charles Lytton is one of the elegant sportsmen (and women) at the ski resort of Cortina D'Ampezzo. Also present is the dazzling Princess Dala, complete with her equally dazzling and pricey jewel, the Pink Panther.

The aristocratic Sir Charles is none other than the notorious jewel thief known as The Phantom and his attention is directed towards ice other than that to be found on the ski slopes.

Hot on The Phantom's trail is bungling police inspector Jacques Clouseau, quite unaware that his wife Simone is actually The Phantom's accomplice.

Sir Charles engages the confidence of the Princess by a ruse and is poised to swoop on the Pink Panther when the opportunity offers, but he is suddenly joined by nephew George, also anxious to lay hands on the jewel.

The action switches to the Princess's Rome villa and during a masked ball both Charles and George make their move to sieze the prey—neither succeeds but the Pink Panther disappears.

Clouseau is now aware of Sir Charles's identity and arrests nephew and uncle. At the trial the defence is that the real Phantom is none other than Clouseau—and the Pink Panther falls out of his pocket.

With Capucine.

With Claudia Cardinale.

Clouseau goes to jail while Sir Charles, George and Simone head for South America. They have little doubt that Clouseau will be released from jail as soon as The Phantom strikes again.

NOTES

The film allowed David Niven to resurrect his old characterisation of 'Raffles' but again he was frustrated. The picture stood or fell upon the farcical performance of Peter Sellers as the detective, and director Blake Edwards used every trick in the annals of screen comedy to accommodate him.

This meant that the plot was left to take care of itself, becoming quite incomprehensible at times, and the story resolved itself into a series of music-hall turns for Sellers.

Sellers carried them off to the complete satisfaction of the *News of the World*. 'I never thought someone would steal a picture from that old professional smoothie David Niven,' wrote their man. 'But it's happened, so help me.'

The *Saturday Review* enjoyed the picture, too. 'I haven't seen a more entertaining film in years.'

Those unwilling to judge the film exclusively as a one-man-show were less enthusiastic.

'David Niven's character has the basis of being a marvellous send-up of all the classy cads in fiction but neither the star nor the director seems to have quite the energy to do it,' said the *Observer*.

The *Daily Express* found Niven supplying 'debonair dash' and the *Sun* saw him 'positively swimming in sophistication like an olive in a Martini'.

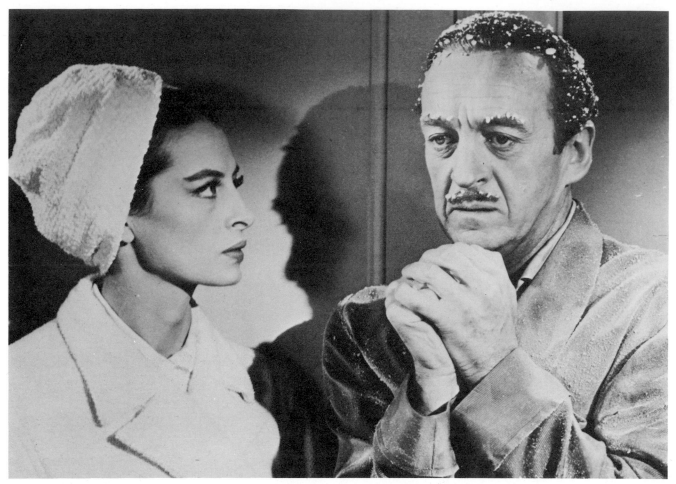

Tense moment with Capucine.

With Robert Wagner.

BEDTIME STORY

1964

A Lankershim-Pennebaker Production. *Producer*: Stanley Shapiro. *Director*: Ralph Levy. *Executive Producer*: Robert Arthur. *Script*: Stanley Shapiro, Paul Henning. *Camera*: Clifford Stine. *Music*: Hans J. Salter. *Editor*: Milton Carruth. *Art*: Alexander Golitzen, Robert Clatworthy. *Wardrobe*: Jean Louis. *Running time*: 99 minutes. Eastmancolor.

CAST

Marlon Brando . . . . *Fred Benson*
David Niven . . . . *Lawrence Jamieson*
Shirley Jones . . . . *Janet Walker*
Dody Goodman . . . . *Fanny Eubank*
Aram Stephen . . . . *Monsieur Andre*
Parley Baer . . . . *Colonel Williams*
Marie Windsor . . . . *Mrs. Sutton*
Rebecca Sand . . . . *Miss Trumble*
Frances Robinson . . . . *Miss Harrington*
Henry Slate . . . . *Sattler*
Norman Alden . . . . *Dubin*
Susanne Cramer . . . . *Anna Kroeger*
Cynthia Lynn . . . . *Frieda*
Ilze Taurins . . . . *Hilda*
Francine York . . . . *Gina*

STORY

Corporal Fred Benson of the American army, and Lawrence Jamieson of the international playboy corps, may be at opposite ends of the social spectrum but they have one thing in common; they are both con-men specialising in tricking attractive women.

When Fred arrives to poach on Lawrence's Riviera snaring ground Lawrence immediately decides to chase him out, but Fred is not so easy to eliminate. So the two join forces.

After a series of successes they select Janet Walker, an American soap queen, as the next victim. But more than loot is involved in this case. The pair agree that the first to relieve her of 25,000 dollars will be deemed the better man and the other will leave town.

Freddy gains the advantage but instead of fleecing the lady he marries her. She is not much loss to Lawrence, being no tycoon but the penniless winner of a soap queen competition. Freddy and bride leave Lawrence to plan his next coup.

A proposition from Marlon Brando.

NOTES

This picture attracted useful advance publicity both as Marlon Brando's first comedy and for the off-beat pairing of Brando and Niven. And, of course, everyone awaited the expected off-stage collision between the amiable and easy-going Niven and the glowering and unpredictable Brando. However ructions did not materialise and Niven returned speaking of Brando in the friendliest fashion. He did relate one interesting anecdote. It seems that Brando broke a long-established movie convention; that film actors have male stand-ins. Brando appointed a girl stand-in.

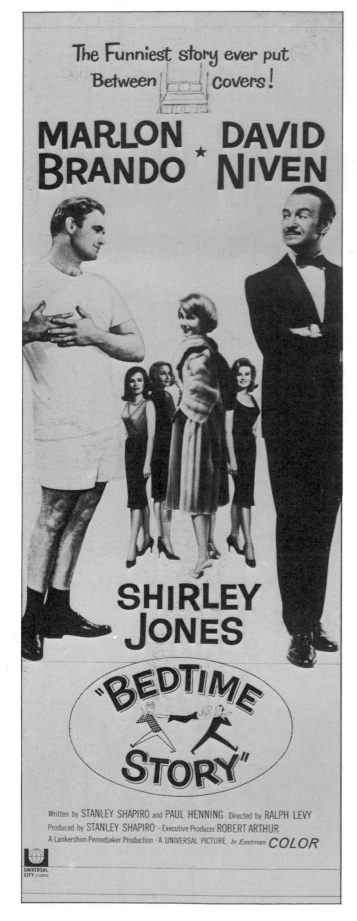

The Funniest story ever put Between covers!

MARLON BRANDO ★ DAVID NIVEN

SHIRLEY JONES

"BEDTIME STORY"

Written by STANLEY SHAPIRO and PAUL HENNING Directed by RALPH LEVY
Produced by STANLEY SHAPIRO · Executive Producer ROBERT ARTHUR
A Lankershim-Pennebaker Production · A UNIVERSAL PICTURE In Eastman COLOR

UNIVERSAL CITY STUDIOS

Niven in familiar role. Brando breaking into comedy.

190

Everyone expected clashes between the two widely differing stars. As this off-set picture shows, all was cordiality (with Shirley Jones).

The film itself was controversial enough, dividing critic against critic both on the merits of Brando as comic and the acceptability of some of the picture's sick jokes.

The lady from the *Observer* was so carried away with general disgust that she ended her review: 'The film was shot, unfortunately not fatally, by Clifford Stine.'

The *Saturday Review* referred to Paul Henning—the co-scriptwriter, and notorious as the creator of TV's *The Beverly Hillbillies*—in the course of a lengthy attack on the film and the principles underlying it, as follows:

'No line or situation is too corny for Henning for he has a heartfelt faith in the ability of the American public to laugh at anything that is obvious.'

The writer was equally cutting about the other scriptwriter and producer, Stanley Shapiro.

But Niven emerged creditably—as he had done so often in the past—from a film which had many critics seething.

Even the *Saturday Review* wrote: 'As a phoney psychiatrist Niven is polished and accomplished.'

Said the *Sunday Express*: 'If Brando does make heavy going of a misjudged experiment, it is a pleasure to see Mr. Niven gliding through with all the vast reserves of smoothness and subtlety at his command.'

The *Daily Express* called the picture 'the most vulgar and embarrassing film of the year' but observed 'David Niven ... stands quietly by garnering all the chuckles with subtle skill while Brando makes a monkey out of himself'.

Let's be kind to both the stars and sign off with this extract from the review in the *Evening News*.

'That the film still does manage to be fairly entertaining speaks well for the finger-light performances of Niven and Brando.'

With Shirley Jones.

Tempted with Marie Windsor.

With Shirley Jones and Marlon Brando.

LADY L

1965

Concordia–Champion–M.G.M. *Producer*: Carlo Ponti. *Director*: Peter Ustinov. *Script*: Peter Ustinov —*from the novel by* Romain Gary. *Camera*: Henri Alekan. *Music*: Jean Franc-aix. *Sets*: Jean D'Eaubonne, August Capelier. *Costume*: Marcel Escoffier, Jacqueline Guyot. *Editor*: Roger Dwyre. *Special Effects*: Karl Baumgartner. *Running time*: 124 minutes. Eastmancolor/Panavision.

CAST

Sophia Loren	. . . .	*Lady Lendale*
Paul Newman	. . . .	*Armand*
David Niven	. . . .	*Dicky, Lord Lendale*
Claud Dauphin	. . . .	*Inspector Mercier*
Phillipe Noiret	. . . .	*Gerome*
Michel Piccoli	. . . .	*Lecoeur*
Marcel Dalio	. . . .	*Sapper*
Cecil Parker	. . . .	*Sir Percy*
Jean Wiener	. . . .	*Krajewski*
Daniel Emilfork	. . . .	*Kobeleff*
Eugene Deckers	. . . .	*Koenigstein*
Jacques Dufilho	. . . .	*Beala*
Tanya Lopert	. . . .	*Agneau*
Catherine Allegret	. . . .	*Pantoufle*
Peter Ustinov	. . . .	*Prince Otto*

STORY

The famous and fabulous widow Lady L (Lady Lendale) is celebrating her 80th birthday with an opulent party for the more opulent of society at her palatial Georgian home in a corner of rural England.

Sir Percy, who is to write her biography, is one of the guests and Lady L escorts him to her summer house and begins to recount the story of her life.

We are wafted back to the year 1900 where Lady L, then simple Louise, is a laundress catering for the staff of a highly sophisticated brothel. She is frequently invited to join the establishment in a more creative capacity but always refuses. She is waiting for the right man to come along. He arrives in the shape of Armand, an idealist who robs to help the poor and later becomes an anarchist. As lovers they live on the trot between Armand's escapades and escaping from Inspector Mercier, a policeman devoted to his capture.

Louise tires of this hectic existence and demands that Armand settles down. He refuses although she is now pregnant. Louise leaves him and travels to Nice where, pretending to be a widowed countess, she meets the fabulously rich and extravagantly eccentric English aristocrat, Lord Lendale. He proposes marriage, happy to be a father to her child. Louise accepts.

The couple settle down at his stately home. Armand arrives on the scene a few years later and demands that Lady Lendale throws a party for her rich friends so that he may conveniently rob them. This plan is foiled by the arrival of the assiduous Inspector Mercier. Armand disappears again.

We return to the present, the party and an explosively surprising finale.

NOTES

M.G.M. had a hard time getting this film off the ground. It was scheduled to star Tony Curtis, Gina Lollobrigida and Sir Ralph Richardson with George Cukor directing. Troubles with the script delayed production so long that the intended stars and director dropped out. Peter Ustinov, in fact, was called in to do a rescue job on a very recalcitrant subject.

He produced something magnificent to look at, packed with some splendid typically Ustinov jokes and set-pieces, gently satirising the upper classes, and a lot of wild puns to elaborate the slim-line story.

Sophia Loren's country house exteriors were shot at Castle Howard with a great deal of enthusiastic help from some of the local gentry as extras.

With Sophia Loren . . . as docile husband.

Sophia Loren, as the French laundress who becomes Lady L, with Paul Newman, the anarchistic Armand.

Peter Ustinov told me an anecdote when I visited Castle Howard during the filming suggesting that although the story belonged to the past the satire did not.

One of the lordly extras asked him: 'Do you put the camera just anywhere?' Answered Ustinov: 'I put the camera where I think it ought to be.' After a weighty pause the man asked: 'Do you put it there yourself or do you have a man do it?'

The critics soon tired of the novelty of seeing an 80-year-old Sophia Loren, scoffed mightily at the casting of Paul Newman as a French anarchist and fretted at the length of the picture. But most of them found Niven a redeeming virtue.

'There is a vintage performance from David Niven as a sad cynic of a lord...' said the *Daily Express*.

'David Niven, unchallenged seigneur of the cosmic domain that lies between a smile and a wince,' said the *Observer*.

'Mr. Niven has infused feeling into what is essentially an exercise in light-hearted absurdity,' said the *Sunday Times*.

The *Daily Mail* noted that the actor's '... belated entrance lifts the film appreciably' and the *Saturday Review*, in harsh mood, observed: 'David Niven is, of course, believable as a lord but unfortunately is given few believable lines as well as an unbelievable character.'

197

WHERE THE SPIES ARE

1965

A Val Guest Production. *Producers*: Val Guest, Steven Pallos. *Director*: Val Guest. *Script*: Val Guest, Wolf Mankowitz, James Leasor—*from* James Leasor's *novel* Passport to Oblivion. *Camera*: Arthur Grant. *Music*: Mario Nascimbene. *Editor*: Bill Lenny. *Art*: John Howell. *Costumes*: Beatrice Dawson. *Running time*: 113 minutes. Metrocolor/Panavision.

CAST

David Niven . . . . *Dr. Jason Love*
Françoise Dorleac . . . . *Vikki*
Cyril Cusack . . . . *Rosser*
John le Mesurier . . . . *MacGillivray*
Nigel Davenport . . . . *Parkington*
Eric Pohlmann . . . . *Farouk*
Paul Stassino . . . . *Simmias*
Ronald Radd . . . . *Stanislaus*
Noel Harrison . . . . *Jackson*
George Pravda . . . . *Agent*

STORY

Out in the Middle East trouble is brewing but British intelligence agent Rosser is eliminated by the opposition before he can transmit the vital information to London.

Being short of available staff to investigate, MacGillivray, head of M.I.5., has to send for an amateur, country doctor Jason Love. Love experienced intelligence work while serving in World War II.

Persuaded to volunteer, Love travels to Rome to meet his first contact, the glamorous Vikki. Delaying for a little more contact with Vikki he misses his plane, which blows up shortly after take-off.

Finally reaching Beirut intact, he is joined by another agent, Parkington. Between them they discover the secret: a plot to assassinate the pro-British Prince of Zaklouf during a state visit to the Lebanon. Despite romantic tangles with Vikki, who turns up again, Love foils the assassination attempt but is snatched by Russian agents in a helicopter.

In the hands of Russian agents (with Françoise Dorleac).

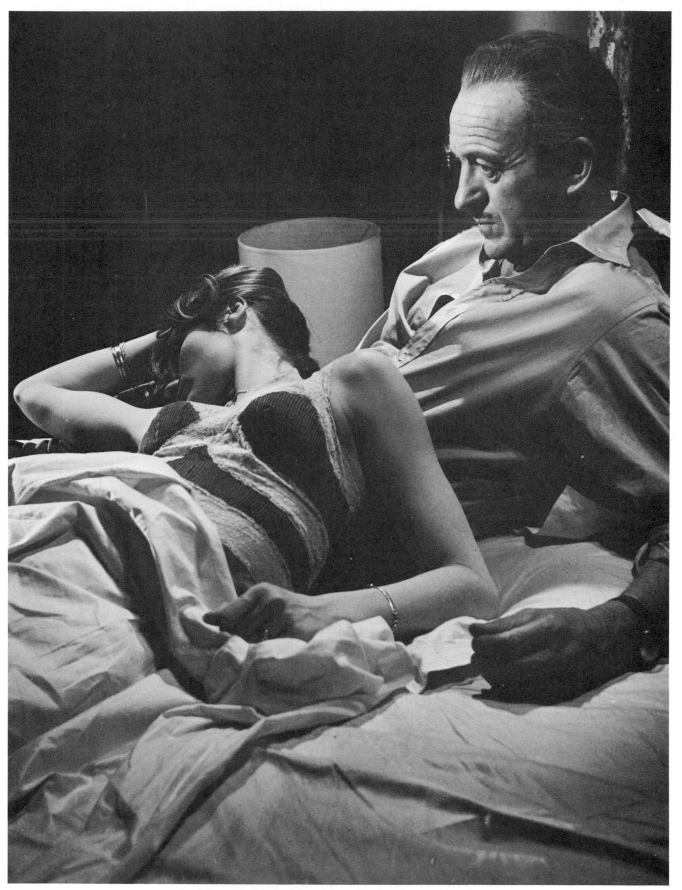

In the world of James Bond, but this secret agent had heart.

He is transferred to a Russian plane and given some rather nasty treatment, a double-agent is un-masked but comes up trumps and Love makes his escape with considerable agility.

NOTES

This was the height of the Bond-inspired spy-mania season in the cinema and David Niven was expected to follow with more adventures of Dr. Jason Love. By the time this one appeared, though, the fashion was on the wane and no sequels materialised.

As might be expected Niven injected a great deal more credibility into the spy hero than was found in most on exhibition at the time.

Alexander Walker summed up his contribution aptly in the *Evening Standard*.

'A vintage star as engagingly witty and implausibility-proof as Mr. Niven is worth any Bond-man's arsenal of booby-trapped accessories and machine-made death traps. I welcome him like a flesh-and-blood transfusion in a kind of film that is now tottering under the weight of its own gimmickry.'

And the *Sunday Express* found: 'Mr. Niven's sure-fire comedy instinct and perfectionist timing are a source of perpetual joy and delight.'

The *Financial Times* said: 'The light comedy sang-froid of this most professional and deft actor amusingly off-sets the bloody adventures into which he is thrown.'

Time approved of him: 'Droll indeed as a middle-aged physician...'

'Mr. Niven simply doesn't give a performance which is less than excellent,' said the *Sunday Times* and the *Daily Mail* pointed out:

'What I really like about Mr. Niven's Dr. Jason Love is that he really seems to care when a colleague is killed. In short, a James Bond with a heart.'

With Françoise Dorleac.

EYE OF THE DEVIL

1966

Filmways—M.G.M. *Producer*: Martin Ransohoff, John Calley. *Director*: J. Lee Thompson. *Script*: Robin Estridge, Dennis Murphy *from* Philip Loraine's *book* Day of the Arrow. *Camera*: Erwin Hillier. *Editor*: Ernest Walters. *Art*: Elliot Scott. *Music*: Gary McFarland. *Costumes*: Julie Harris. *Running time*: 90 minutes.

CAST

Deborah Kerr . . . . *Catherine de Montfaucon*
Davin Niven . . . . *Philippe de Montfaucon*
Donald Pleasence . . . . . *Père Dominic*
Edward Mulhare . . . . . . *Jean-Claude Ibert*
Flora Robson . . . . *Countess Estelle*
Emlyn Williams . . . . . . *Alain de Montfaucon*
Sharon Tate . . . . *Odile*
David Hemmings . . . . . *Christian de Caray*
John le Mesurier . . . . . . *Dr. Monnet*
Suky Appleby . . . . *Antoinette*
Donald Bisset . . . . *Rennard*

STORY

Life seems to be going swimmingly for Philippe de Montfaucon, wife Catherine and son Alain, until a mysterious retainer arrives from his country estates with the news that the grape harvest has failed.

Looking rather more dejected than even this bad news would seem to warrant, Philippe leaves at once for the chateau.

It turns out to be a curious place. The servants are fretful, the resident Countess Estelle distraught and the local priest Père Dominic grave. Oddity is compounded by the presence of a strange youth, who wreaks havoc on the local bird life with a bow and arrow, and an equally strange maid who appears to have sinister magical powers.

Alarmed by a dream, Catherine takes her son off to the chateau to ensure that all is well. She becomes embroiled in a nightmare of frightening incidents; men in hoods and cowls taking part in secret ceremonies and sacrifices depleting the local bird life still further, among them.

With Deborah Kerr.

This film was pretty punishing for all concerned (with Sharon Tate)

In the end she discovers the whole set-up is a nest of Satanists who habitually sacrifice the willing head of the Montfaucon clan when the grapes let them down. The deed is duly done and Catherine hurries away determined to remove her son permanently from such nasty habits but he has already made his compact....

NOTES

The eye of the devil seemed to have been glinting evilly upon this project from the start. The leading lady, Kim Novak, was injured in a riding accident during filming and was replaced by Deborah Kerr. This landed the film company with the cost of re-shooting eight weeks completed work. David Niven remarked sadly at the time what a strain it was working up the dramatic juices second time around and this may at least partly account for his total inability on this occasion to give the film any helping hand towards survival.

'David Niven is steeped in witchcraft down at the family chateau. He looks pained, perhaps because of the dialogue, perhaps because of the absurdities,' said the usually amiable *News of the World*.

'Hilariously bad,' was the verdict of the *Sunday Times*.

David Niven in the hands of Satan and a preposterous script.

CASINO ROYALE

1967

With Ursula Andress and a host of
stars, Niven joined in a muddled
effort of send up the spy saga.

A Famous Artists Production. *Producers*: Charles K. Feldman, Jerry Bresler, *Directors*: John Huston, Ken Hughes, Val Guest, Robert Parrish, Joe McGrath, Richard Talmadge, Anthony Squire. *Script*: Wolf Mankowitz, John Law, Michael Sayers—*from the* Ian Fleming *novel. Camera*: Jack Hildyard, John Wilcox, Nicholas Roeg. *Designer*: Michael Stringer. *Costume*: Julie Harris. *Editor*: Bill Lenny. *Art*: John Howell, Ivor Beddoes, Lionel Couch. *Music*: Burt Bacharach. *Running time*: 131 minutes. Technicolor/Panavision.

CAST

Peter Sellers . . . . *Evelyn Tremble*
Ursula Andress . . . . *Vesper Lynd*
David Niven . . . . *Sir James Bond*
Orson Welles . . . . *Le Chiffre*
Joanna Pettet . . . . *Mata Bond*
Daliah Lavi . . . . *Detainer*
Woody Allen . . . . *Jimmy Bond*
Deborah Kerr . . . . *Mimi*
William Holden . . . . *Ransome*
Charles Boyer . . . . *Le Grand*
John Huston . . . . *M*
Kurt Kaszner . . . . *Smernov*
George Raft . . . . *as himself*
Jean Paul Belmondo . . . . *Legionnaire*
Terence Cooper . . . . *Cooper*
Barbara Bouchet . . . . *Moneypenny*
and many other familiar faces

STORY

The story defies explanation. Sir James Bond, the real article, not to be confused with any flashy imitations, is brought out of retirement by M to fight the dreaded SMERSH. His first assignment is in the Highlands, coping with such things as exploding haggis, and fighting off SMERSH agent Mimi and her glamorous houris. Action is piled on action as we meet numerous James Bonds not overlooking the son of Bond and the daughter of Bond as well. The adventures conclude in a holocaust of special effects.

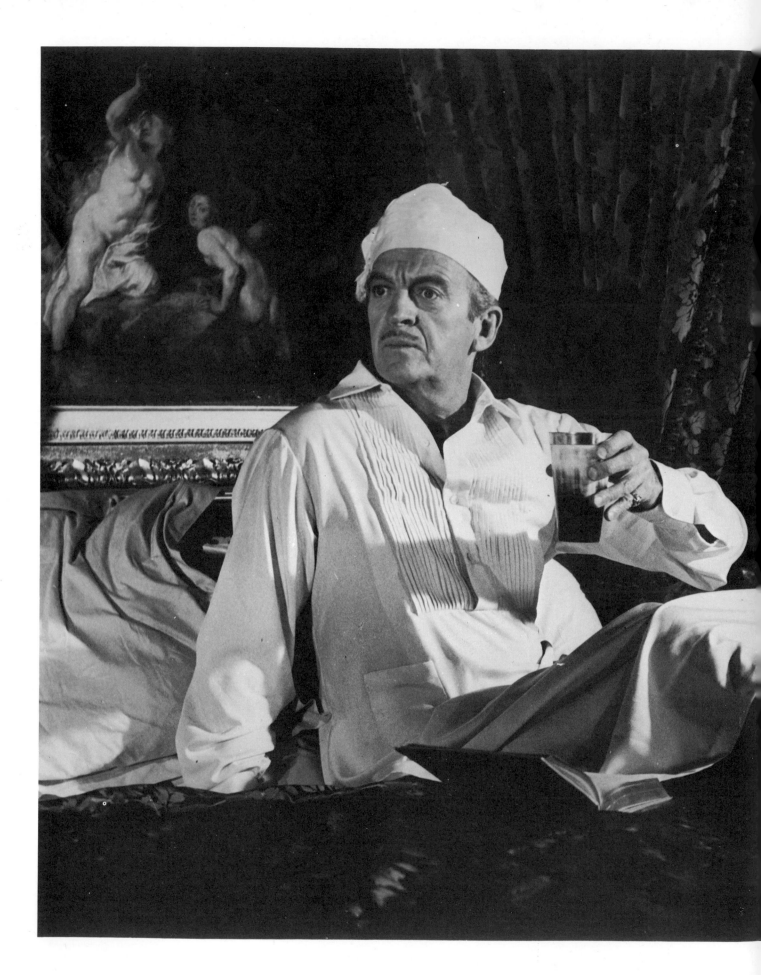

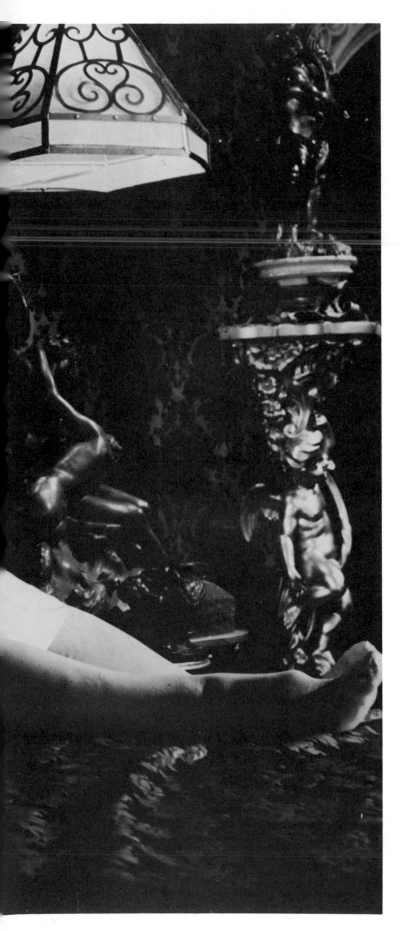

NOTES

Lacking Sean Connery, the authentic screen Bond of the time, the producers elected to do a send-up of a normal Bond film as a sort of substitute. It seems that the scheme, with six directors participating, grew increasingly out of hand and the finished article resembled a sea of star faces in perpetual tumult.

The film gleaned valuable publicity during production by making a big secret of who, out of a huge cast, was actually playing James Bond. I remember asking David Niven at the time the usual asinine questions on the subject and his face was a furrowed picture of despair as he tried to maintain both his usual honesty and loyalty to his employers.

As it turns out not even intelligent questions were worth asking or answering. With the usual compliance of the press, who love talking in vast sums, the budget of the picture was discussed in astronomical terms. It was, without doubt, hugely costly (one studio was not big enough to hold it) and although it was reasonably successful with the public here (but not in America) it is doubtful if it ever recovered its cost.

The critics wound it unceremoniously through the mangle. One of the more kindly was Donald Zec, in the *Daily Mirror*. 'I think I can honestly say, with my hand on my stomach, that *Casino Royale* is the worst film I ever enjoyed,' he wrote.

'A big, colourful, noisy star-studded, plot-less junk pile of a mess,' pronounced the *Guardian*.

The *Evening News* deplored the waste of money when good films couldn't get finance.

Generally the acting performances were flayed along with the picture, but almost the sole exception was David Niven, magically keeping his head above the syrup.

'David Niven stays scrupulous to the end,' said the *Sunday Telegraph*, 'but in Peter Sellers, Woody Allen, Orson Welles, Deborah Kerr, we see symptoms of the self-cherishing which presumes audiences to be comprised entirely of autograph hunters.'

'David Niven plays with his usual polish,' said the *Daily Telegraph*. 'David Niven and Deborah Kerr hit just the right note of extravagant absurdity,' said *The Times*.

'It is only David Niven ... who betrays any real sense of comedy,' noted *Playboy*.

The egregious Andrew Sarris was, of course, the odd man out and seeming to nurse a neurotic animosity towards the aged wrote in *Village Voice*: 'I don't like *Casino Royale,* particularly when John Huston is flaunting the hardened arteries of David Niven and Deborah Kerr in a Scottish castle.'

As Sir James Bond,
with nightcaps.

209

Lunacy with Barbara Bouchet.

Niven was about the only redeeming feature of *Casino Royale* despite the presence (seen here) of John Huston (who also had a hand in the directing) and William Holden, Charles Boyer and Kurt Kaszner.

Froth . . . and plenty of pretty girls represented a major part of the picture.

THE EXTRAORDINARY SEAMAN

1968

John Frankenheimer Productions—Edward Lwis Productions for M.G.M. *Producer*: Edward Lewis. *Co-producer*: John H. Cushingham. *Script*: Phillip Rock, Hal Dresner—*from a story by* Phillip Rock. *Camera*: Lionel Lindon. *Music*: Maurice Jarre. *Art*: George W. Davies, Edward Carfagno. *Running time*: 80 minutes. Metrocolor/Panavision.

CAST

David Niven . . . . . . *Lt. Commander Finchhaven R.N.*

Faye Dunaway . . . . *Jennifer Winslow*
Alan Alda . . . . . . *Lt. J. G. Morton Krim*
Mickey Rooney . . . . *Cook 3/c W. G. Oglethorpe*
Jack Carter . . . . . . *Gunner's Mate Orville Toole*
Juano Hernandez . . . *Ali Shar*
Manu Tupou . . . . . *Sean I/C Lightfoot Star*
Barry Kelly . . . . . . *Admiral Barnwell*
Leonard O. Smith . . *Dyak*
Richard Guizon . . . . *Dyak*
John Cochran . . . . . *Dyak*
Jerry Fujikawa . . . . *Admiral Shimagoshi*

STORY

Four American seamen, adrift in World War II off the Philippines, float ashore. Exploring the terrain they come across Lt. Commander Finchhaven and speedily realise he's British because he's lustily singing Gilbert and Sullivan.

He's near a ship aground on a sandbank. Finchhaven explains that it is a Royal Navy ship abandoned by its crew. If they will help him get it refloated he promises to transport them to Australia—if they will act as crew.

A deal is done. Needing batteries to start the engine, the party raid a deserted village. They find the batteries, and their owner, a blonde beauty Jennifer Winslow. She hands them over, in return for passage with the crew.

When, after sundry adventures, the team reach the open sea they discover their captain has the crazy notion to sink a Jap cruiser.

He then confesses he is a ghost who fell dead drunk on his first engagement and had been sent back from the beyond by outraged seagoing ancestors to redeem the honour of the line.

The senior American, Lt. Krim, manages to get his shipmates away safely from the ship—but he and Jennifer fail to make it. They finally decide to help Finchhaven—if you can't beat 'em sink with 'em.

They succeed in the mad mission. But the war is already over. Finchhaven had botched another job and must linger in his watery limbo.

NOTES

A change of uniform and a chance to work with director Frankenheimer were two attractions here for David Niven. Unhappily this was not the variable Frankenheimer at his best. It used a lot of newsreel and similar insertions, many of them joked up, to emphasise an anti-war message. Most of the critics ignored it and the distributors didn't push it.

Majorie Bilbow in *Today's Cinema* found it confusing and wrote: 'A cleverly made curiosity, not so much produced as manufactured' and found the interpolated material not only got between the viewer and story

but edged out the stars. 'Anyone looking forward to David Niven, Faye Dunaway and Mickey Rooney will be sadly disappointed.'

The *BFI Bulletin* recorded: 'Compressed to 80 minutes the film often takes on the appearance of a pop art collage ... the satire of war works at a fairly simple level of enjoyable buffoonery.'

As insubstantial skipper.

PRUDENCE AND THE PILL

1968

Twentieth Century Fox. *Producers*: Kenneth Harper, Ronald Kahn. *Directors*: Fielder Cook; Ronald Neame. *Script*: Hugh Mills—*from his novel. Camera*: Ted Moore. *Design*: Wilfred Shingleton. *Editor*: Norman Sawage. *Costumes*: Julie Harris. *Music*: Bernard Ebbinghouse. *Art*: Fred Carter. *Running time*: 92 minutes. De Luxe Color.

CAST

Deborah Kerr . . . . *Prudence Hardcastle*
David Niven . . . . *Gerald Hardcastle*
Robert Coote . . . . *Henry Hardcastle*
Irina Demick . . . . *Elizabeth*
Joyce Redman . . . . *Grace Hardcastle*
Judy Geeson . . . . *Geraldine Hardcastle*
Keith Michell . . . . *Dr. Alan Hewitt*
Edith Evans . . . . *Lady Roberta Bates*
David Dundas . . . . *Tony Bates*
Vickery Turner . . . . *Rose*
Hugh Armstrong . . . . *Ted*
Peter Butterworth . . . . . . *Chemist*
Moyra Fraser . . . . *Woman*

STORY

Gerald Hardcastle, chairman of one of the big banks, lives in his English stately home with his wife Prudence. They have endured a gracious, uneventful and chillingly formal married life for twelve years.

Gerald's less stately desires are catered for by his mistress Elizabeth while those of his wife Prudence are prescribed for by her lover Dr. Hewitt.

Gerald's brother Henry and wife, with their 18-year-old daughter Geraldine, live on a more modest level. They catch Geraldine in a suspicious situation with her boyfriend and counsel her on the dangers of pregnancy but Geraldine reassures them—she's on the pill—her mother's.

Henry consults brother Gerald, who discovers as a result that his own wife is on the pill and must therefore have a lover.

With Deborah Kerr.

Niven's expressions off-set during the making of *Prudence and the Pill* . . .

. . . and on-set suggest he was receiving accurate premonitions of its critical reception.

With Christian Roberts and Edith Evans.

Various members of the two households, each with their own complicated motives, indulge in an orgy of switching pills for aspirins.

In the meantime Elizabeth, bored at Gerald's delay in asking his wife for a divorce, leaves him. Prudence goes on a holiday with her lover.

In the end, after due process of divorce, Gerald marries Elizabeth, Prudence marries her doctor. Geraldine marries her boy-friend. Soon almost every woman in sight is pregnant. The film ends not so much with a whimper as a population explosion.

NOTES

The *New York Times* summed up this unfortunate film in this comment upon the performers: 'Because their parts are unendurable they give the worst, worst performances of their lives.'

The *Saturday Review* was kinder: 'Deborah Kerr and David Niven, two impeccable professionals, know exactly when and how to raise an elegant eyebrow, to deliver a poisonous sally. Because of this they impart an aura of propriety and taste to what could otherwise have been a leering, tasteless mess.'

Time snapped: 'This cretinous comedy . . .'

'A few spurts of gaiety are supplied by the elegance and distinction of Mr. Niven', said the *Sunday Times,* but the *Daily Telegraph* wrote wearily: 'David Niven playing the owner of an atrociously over-decorated period house . . . is reduced eventually to pulling funny faces.'

Niven and Kerr: on screen an icy partnership.

THE IMPOSSIBLE YEARS

1968

Marten Productions Inc. Picture. *Producer*: Lawrence Weingarten. *Director*: Michael Gordon. *Script*: George Wells—*from the play by* Bob Fisher, Arthur Marx. *Camera*: William H. Daniels. *Music*: Don Costa. *Art*: George W. Davis, Preston Ames. *Editor*: James E. Newcom. *Running time*: 98 minutes. Metrocolor/Panavision.

CAST

David Niven . . . . *Jonathan Kingsley*
Lola Albright . . . . *Alice Kingsley*
Chad Everett . . . . *Richard Merrick*
Ozzie Nelson . . . . *Dr. Herbert Fleischer*
Christina Ferrare . . . . . . *Linda Kingsley*
Jeff Cooper . . . . *Bartholomew Smuts*
John Harding . . . . *Dean Harvey Rockwell*
Richard Chalet . . . . *Freddie Fleischer*
Mike McGreevey . . . . . . *Andy McLaine*
Don Beddoe . . . . *Dr. Elliot Fish*
Darleen Carr . . . . *Abbey Kingsley*
Louise Lorimer . . . . *Mrs. Celia Fish*
Karen Norris . . . . *Mrs. Rockwell*
Susan French . . . . *Miss Hammer*
Trudi Ames . . . . *Francine*
Edward McKinley . . . . . . *Dr. Pepperell*
Ned Wertimer . . . . *Dr. Bodey*

STORY

Dr. Jonathan Kingsley is a psychiatrist specialising in teenager management. While lecturing his class on the subject at the university he learns that his own 17-year-old daughter Linda has been arrested for picketing her college.

Anxious to put his own house in order the doctor, after bailing his daughter out, rebukes her for general sloppiness and bad school records and diagnoses that the roots of her disorder lie in seeing too much of Freddie, the boy next door. She should enlarge her circle.

She responds by filling the house with way-outs and weirdies, among them a beatnik painter. Consternation is caused when a nude picture of Linda, painted by the artist, is discovered.

The general commotion is holding up work on Dr. Kingsley's new book, so he consents to Linda and her mob going off to celebrate July 4th together. She returns looking clean, respectable and decorous. She has been reformed through marriage.

Fearing her father will have the marriage annulled she refuses to divulge the name of the groom. As it turns out to be the doctor's clean limbed friend Richard, Kingsley and wife give the union their blessing.

Generation gap. As father with daughter Christina Ferrare.

Jeff Cooper as visiting hippie.

There were few scenes to laugh at in *The Impossible Years* but this sequence with Chad Everett was one of them.

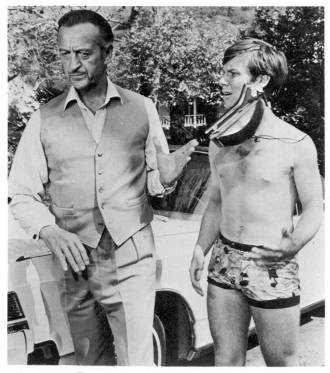

Frustration with Mike McGreevey.

Harmony with Lola Albright.

Unhappily in the thick of the teenage scene.

NOTES

The reader will already have noticed we are not enjoying one of David Niven's golden periods. In fact, his career at this time, depending how academic you care to be, could be described as in a state of recession or downright slump.

This dreadful film—a Hollywood comedy of 'the generation gap' which didn't bridge it but fell right into it—does not even represent rock bottom, as worse is to come, although *The Times* found it 'Of a dreariness which not even the usually saving presence of David Niven and Lola Albright, as the troubled parents, can alleviate.'

'Not even David Niven, adept though he usually is at enlivening a dull comedy, can coax much laughter out of film as stubbornly unfunny,' lamented the *Daily Mail*.

'Even old Niven can't pull anything but a very dead rabbit out of the hat,' said the *Evening News,* putting candour before grace.

'David Niven in his worst ever film,' snapped *The People*.

Variety, however, rallied round: 'David Niven stars in a good performance matched by the entire cast.'

The Impossible Years and an impossible task for Niven.

221

BEFORE WINTER COMES

1969

A Windward Production. *Producer*: Robert Emmett Ginna. *Director*: J. Lee Thompson. *Script*: Andrew Sinclair *from the story by* Frederick L. Keefe. *Camera*: Gil Taylor. *Music*: Ron Grainer. *Art*: John Blezard. *Editor*: Willy Kemplen. *Running time*: 103 minutes. Technicolor.

CAST

David Niven . . . . *Major Burnside*
Topol . . . . *Janovic*
Anna Karina . . . . *Maria*
John Hurt . . . . *Lt. Pilkington*
Anthony Quayle . . . . *Brigadier Bewley*
Ori Levy . . . . *Kamenev*
John Collin . . . . *Sgt. Woody*
George Innes . . . . *Bill*
Hugh Futcher . . . . *Joe*
Tony Selby . . . . *Ted*
Colin Spaull . . . . *Alf*
Christopher Sandford . . . . *Johnny*
Larry Dann . . . . *Al*
Karel Stepanek . . . . *Count Kerassy*
Guy Deghy . . . . *Kovacs*
Mark Malicz . . . . *Komenski*
Gertan Klauber . . . . *Russian major*
Hana-Marea Pravda . . . . *Beata*
Jeffrey Wickham . . . . *Captain Roots*
Constantine De Goguel . . . . . *Russian corporal*

STORY

At the end of World War II it is the job of British officer Major Giles Burnside to establish a camp in Austria for displaced persons. It is one of his tasks to decide whether the refugees should be sent to East or West.

Janovic, a refugee with thirteen languages, is made official interpreter and unofficially takes over much of the running of the camp. Burnside doesn't relish the job and is occupied, anyway, with courting Maria, one of the local girls. But he has competition in Janovic.

Janovic is revealed as a Russian deserter. Under an Allied agreement he must be returned home—and to execution.

Burnside puts him in a truck for transportation to the West, but it actually heads for the Russian lines.

NOTES

David Niven rejoined J. Lee Thompson again for another excursion to Europe and this time the trip had a more rewarding outcome.

Before Winter Comes attempted to combine a vehicle for the rumbustious Topol with some deep thinking on the subject of duty and conscience. It didn't come off on either level and the reception was mixed.

Dilys Powell in the *Sunday Times* was in no doubt that the film was a triumph for the leading man.

Once more in uniform, a spate of idiotic comedies behind him, Niven regained dignity in this picture (seen with John Hurt).

With Topol.

'Mr. Niven has had some pretty shaggy roles of late; good to see this beautiful actor given a chance to extend his range. He subdues his natural charm in the portrait of military correctness, but gradually lets you see the man becoming involved, shaken by the possibility of mistakes; at last you recognise his loneliness trapped in the intolerable position of command.'

The *Daily Mail* reported: 'David Niven wavering subtly between impersonal military authority and personal weakness.'

'David Niven, as impeccable as ever, but in solemn vein,' said the *Observer*.

The *Sun,* not liking the picture, conceded: 'Niven excelled as the major.'

Time was unimpressed: 'Vague plot, conventional camera-work, and a feeble scenario.' *The Times* ('David Niven has a certain weary dignity') and the *Daily Telegraph* ('David Niven's major is pleasantly dry') were also among the unimpressed but Niven, saddled with unsatisfactory films at this time, needed some kind words to boost his ego—and he got them.

LE CERVEAU

(Anglo-U.S.A. title : THE BRAIN)

1969

Gaumont International–Dino de Laurentiis Production. *Producer*: Alain Poiré. *Director*: Gerard Oury. *Script*: Gerard Oury, Marcel Jullian, Daniel Thompson. *Art*: Jean Andre. *Music*: Georges Delerue. *Running time*: 100 minutes. Eastmancolor/Franscope.

CAST

David Niven . . . . *The Brain*
Jean-Paul Belmondo. . . . . *Arthur*
Bourvil . . . . *Anatole*
Eli Wallach . . . . *Scannapieco*
Silvia Monti . . . . *Sofia*
Fernand Gerome. . . . . *The Commissaire*
Jacques Balutin . . . . *Pochet*
Jacques Ciron . . . . *Duboeuf*
Fernand Guiot . . . . *Mazurel*

STORY

The Brain is a gentleman master criminal and the man behind the British Great Train Robbery (also a colonel in the British Army). He is now planning another similar operation, to snatch NATO's entire military funds (12 million dollars) while they are being transported by train from Paris to Brussels. It helps when he is put in charge of the train's security. But two small-time crooks, Arthur and Anatole, are planning the same caper. Despite The Brain's massively planned operation it is Arthur and Anatole who actually get away with the loot. The Brain gets it back but then both he and the haul are kidnapped by some of the local mafiosi. Arthur and Anatole keep in pursuit and so do the police.

The Brain, in the end, turns the tables on them all

In French farce, sixties style.

In *The Brain* a full colonel in the British Army....

... also a gentleman crook who, says the story, master-minded the Great British Train Robbery.

but just fails in his final ploy—to transport the cash to America in a huge replica of the Statue of Liberty.

NOTES

This was a French example of one of the new cinematic novelties: the frenetic comedy style of the Keystone Cops era adapted to fit the tastes of the sixties. Lacking any hint of the classic simplicity of the originals they were as confusing as they were unfunny.

David Niven worked hard to make this one work—even playing each scene in English and then repeating it in French as well as helping, no doubt, to attract the American dollars invested in the picture.

'Niven's lines are given a martini-like delivery,' said *Time*. 'In a sorry season *The Brain* is smart enough to pass for comedy.'

The *Daily Mail* pronounced that he had 'a suavity that survives every humiliation, including being locked in a trunk, tossed fully clothed into a swimming-pool and half-drowned in a flooded bathroom.'

The *New Statesman* said: 'David Niven doing pratfalls and allowing his barbered and pampered face to undergo indignities gives unexpected slapstick value.'

But with all his professional stops out David Niven could not save this film. 'Deplorable waste of talent,' said the *Sunday Times*. '*The Brain* needs a transplant in the script department,' said the *Daily Sketch*.

THE STATUE

1970

Josef Shaftel Production. *Producer*: Anis Nohra. *Executive Producer*: Josef Shaftel. *Director*: Rod Amateau. *Script*: Alec Coppel, Denis Norden—*from* Alec Coppel's *play* Chip, Chip, Chip. *Camera*: Piero Portalupi. *Editor*: Ernest Hosler. *Art*: Bruno Avesani. *Music*: Riz Ortolani. *Running time*: 89 minutes. Eastmancolor.

CAST

David Niven . . . . *Alex Bolt*
Virna Lisi . . . . *Rhonda Bolt*
Robert Vaughn . . . . *Ray Whiteley*
Ann Bell . . . . *Pat Demarest*
John Cleese . . . . *Harry*
Tim Brooke-Taylor . . . . *Hillcrest*
Hugh Burden . . . . *Sir Geoffrey*
Erik Chitty . . . . *Mouser*
Derek Francis . . . . *Sanders*
Susan Travers . . . . *Mrs. Southwick*
Desmond Walter-Ellis . . . . *Mr. Southwick*

STORY

Professor Alex Bolt, inventor of a new global language, UNISPEAK, is awarded the Nobel prize for promoting international understanding. This delights Ray Whiteley, power hungry American Ambassador to London, who has backed the professor's new language, strictly in the interests of his political advancement.

Bolt's wife, Rhonda, a sculptress, is persuaded by Whiteley to produce a giant statue of her husband that can stand opposite the American Embassy in Grosvenor Square.

There are shocks all round when the statue is privately previewed—it is starkers. But for Bolt the worst shock is when he observes that a very private part of the statue is clearly not his own.

He tries to get the unveiling stopped while he hunts for the male who posed for the anatomical anomaly (code name: Charlie). As political and international elements are involved almost everything American from the Pentagon to the C.I.A. becomes involved in

With Virna Lisi in a monster-sized hunk of vulgarity.

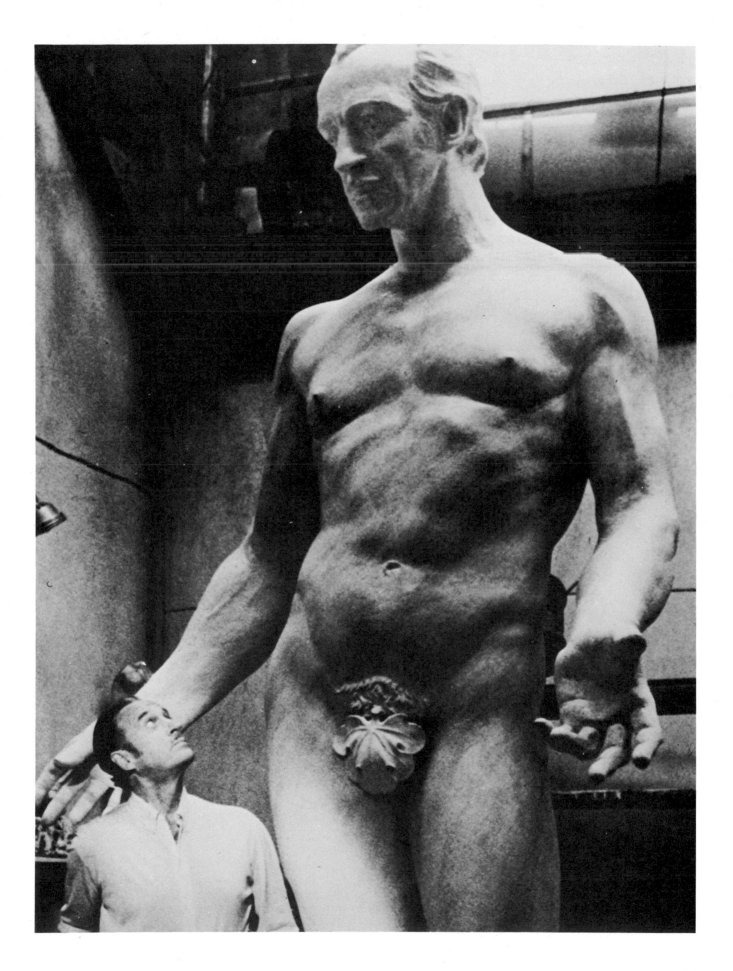

the search.

The hunt for the missing member concludes, with a surprise, amidst the classical purlieus of Italy.

NOTES

No admirer of David Niven would want to loiter around this coy monstrosity. 'I am happy to say that David Niven looks thoroughly uncomfortable about the whole sorry business,' said the *Daily Express*.

'For very simple audiences only,' was the verdict of *The Times*. 'David Niven, poor fellow,' lamented the *Guardian*.

But most films, however bad, can find a friend somewhere. 'Not for prudes, but a fast-moving package of fun,' said William Hall of the *Evening News*.

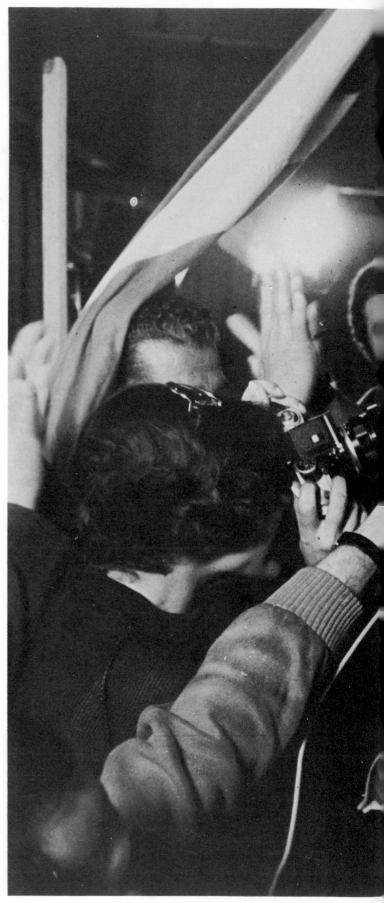

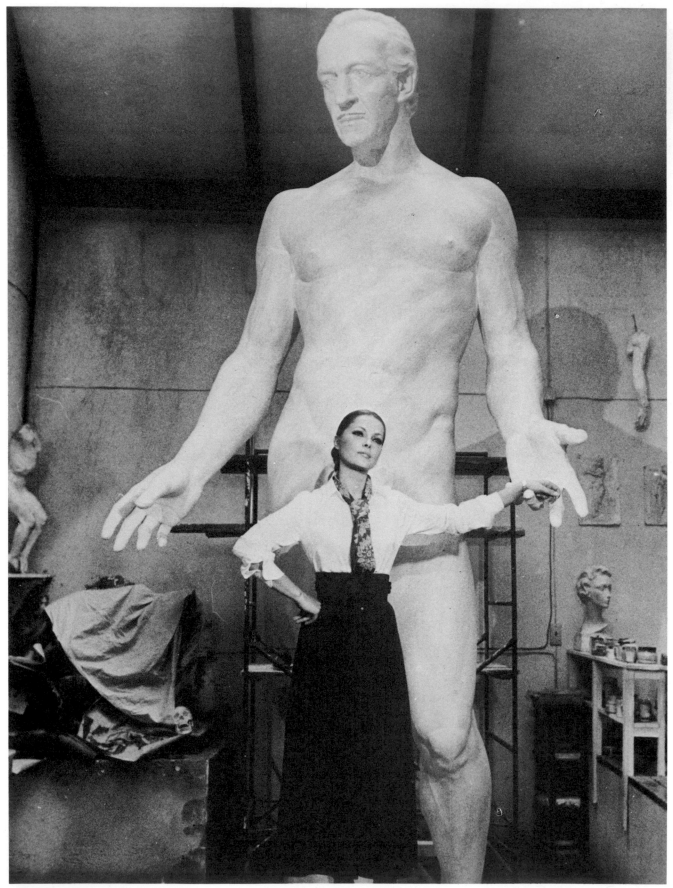

Virna Lisi with her creation.

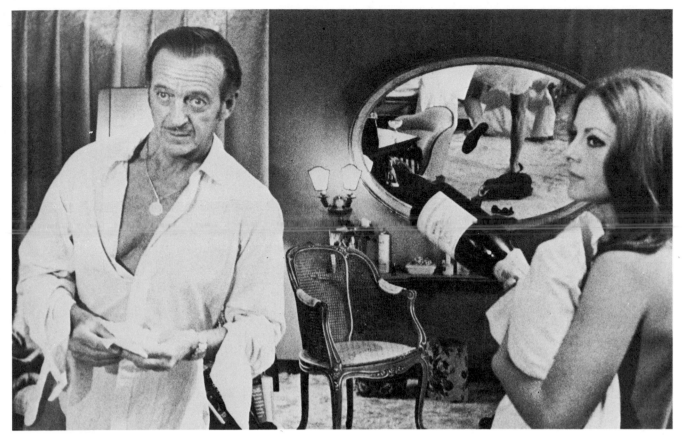

As a Nobel prize winner, would you believe?

With Robert Vaughn.

KING, QUEEN, KNAVE

(Additional title: HERZBUBE)

1972

Maran-Film–Wolper Pictures Ltd. *Producer*: David L. Wolper. *Director*: Jerzy Skolimowski. *Script*: David Seltzer, David Shaw—*from the novel by* Vladimir Nabokov. *Camera*: Charly Steinberger. *Art*: Rolf Zehetbauer. *Editor*: Mel Shapiro. *Costume*: Ina Stein. *Running time*: 92 minutes. Eastmancolor.

CAST

Gina Lollobrigida . . . . *Martha Dreyer*
David Niven . . . . *Charles Dreyer*
John Moulder Brown . . . . *Frank Dreyer*
Mario Adorf . . . . *Ritter*
Carl Fox-Duering . . . . *Entricht*
Christopher Sandford . . . . *Hofmann*
Christine Schuberth . . . . *Isolda*
Felicitas Peters . . . . *Ida*
Erica Beer . . . . *Frieda*
Elma Karlowa . . . . *Hanna*
Morgens von Gadow . . . . *Piffke*

STORY

Frank Dreyer, a 19-year-old, near-sighted, gangling lad innocent in most things and particularly in matters of love, loses his parents in a car crash and leaves Britain to join his uncle, Charles Dreyer, in Germany.

Charles Dreyer, once a dashing World War II army captain, stayed on in Munich after the war and went into shopkeeping. He also married Martha, then a penniless refugee.

Charles has prospered, owning a big store; his wife has expanded in grandeur to match her husband's success. She is frankly contemptuous of young Frank, but she fills him with burning, adolescent sexual yearnings.

Frank makes friends with an eccentric inventor, Ritter, and introduces him to his uncle, who considers the man's inventions practical and profitable. Charles now begins to think of Frank as a potential heir. Martha's

Adding Gina Lollobrigida to his list of internationally famous leading ladies.

236

Niven had great faith in this picture but the distributors cold-shouldered it and the critics were divided.

The passing years. As Charles Dreyer, Niven plays a man who was *once* a dashing World War II army captain.

attitude rapidly adjusts to this change in Frank's fortunes and, unknown to busy Charles, they become lovers and talk of marriage.

A divorce is unlikely so Frank and Martha have a problem. Martha suggests a holiday at the Cote d'Azur and a boating accident ... Charles cannot swim.

The plan is put into effect, though not without qualms of conscience on Frank's part, and one day they are at sea in a small boat and the moment for murder has arrived.

Suddenly Charles reveals that through the success of one of Ritter's inventions he is 250,000 dollars the richer. Martha hesitates, and so does Frank, who has been having second thoughts anyway. But an accident capsizes the boat.

Frank, his glasses lost, can't see. Martha, like Charles, can't swim. She cries for help ... and the affairs of

the king, queen and knave are ready for a surprise solution.

NOTES

This picture by Skolimowski, the Polish director highly thought of in many quarters, did not come up to the expectations of the distributors, particularly as it got a critical drubbing at the Cannes Film Festival. They slipped it out without benefit of a showing to the reviewers although some adventurous spirits caught up with it just the same.

'A plethora of badly timed sexual black comedy,' said the *Guardian*.

'Made with grace and style,' said the *Observer*.

'It would have been hard to predict that David Niven, Gina Lollobrigida and John Moulder Brown would have teamed so brilliantly in Skolimowski's idiosyncratic style of farce,' was the opinion of *The Times*.

238

VAMPIRA

1973

A World Film Services Production. *Producer*: Jack H. Weiner. *Director*: Clive Donner. *Script*: Jeremy Lloyd. *Camera*: Tony Richmond. *Art*: Philip Harrison. *Editor*: Bill Butler. *Music*: David Whitaker. *Costumes*: Vangie Harrison. *Running time*: 89 minutes. Eastmancolor.

CAST

David Niven . . . . *Count Dracula*
Teresa Graves . . . . *Countess Vampira*
Peter Bayliss . . . . *Maltravers*
Jennie Linden . . . . *Angela*
Nicky Henson . . . . *Marc*
Linda Hayden . . . . *Helga*
Bernard Bresslaw . . . . *Pottinger*
Cathie Shirrif . . . . *Nancy*
Andrea Allan . . . . *Eve*
Veronica Carlson . . . . *Ritva*
Minah Bird . . . . *Rose*
Christopher Sandford . . . . . . *Milton*
Freddie Jones . . . . *Gilmore*
Frank Thornton . . . . *Mr. King*

STORY

The Dracula of 1973 is a witty, debonair, English-style gentleman ministered to by Maltravers, his unflappable manservant. But his beloved Countess Dracula is asleep in the depths of their Transylvanian castle awaiting a blood transfusion to restore her to the ranks of the living dead.

The castle is a popular attraction; parties are offered a tour of the building and dinner served by Dracula and a beautiful girl vampire.

A group including the finalists in a *Playboy* 'The Most Biteable Playmate of the Month' competition turn up and Dracula adopts his usual fiendish practice of taking blood samples from all visiting females in his search for the right blood group to resuscitate Vampira. On this occasion he's successful. A transfusion takes place but when Vampira awakes she rapidly turns black.

Due to a mix-up at the sampling stages the Count is unable to pin-point the donor. They follow the party back to London and track down the right girl to give the Countess, it is hoped, a restorative dose.

Dracula Niven style . . . a witty, debonair English gentleman.

After sundry devilish machinations—including gory work at a Playboy Vampire Ball—the right blood is found and pumped into Vampira in the hope of reversing the process.

The result is not the one expected and it has a startling effect on Count Dracula.

NOTES

This second foray into the horror field was better fated than the first—but only just; this one, at least, was intended as a spoof and the central character as a joke.

'What a glorious idea to have the witty David Niven playing a latter-day Count Dracula who grades his blood according to vintages and sips it gracefully out of crystal glasses,' said the *Daily Mail*.

Unfortunately this vein of humour is soon bled dry and most of the film has that frenzied air that served

director Clive Donner in his swinging sixties period. 'The film's humour is asinine,' snapped the *Financial Times* and observed 'The film has been sitting on the distributors' shelves for some time . . .' and hinted that it had only been forced into the cinemas to beat some other spoof horror films on the way, including Andy Warhol's *Blood for Dracula*.

The picture was finished towards the end of 1973 and opened in London in October, 1974, not an inordinately long interval between end of production and première.

'David Niven squanders his elegance on a Dracula-jest,' was the reaction of the *Sunday Times*. The *Observer* didn't care much for the film either but remarked of Niven: 'You would be amazed, would you not, if he didn't do it suavely. But the screenplay is the standard British collection of excuses for persuading a group of not entirely unwatchable females into standard British states of almost-undress . . .'

A comic Dracula was inevitable and Niven the ideal man to play the part but the script soon ran out of wit and into funereal farce.

Sampling the latest vintage.

PAPER TIGER

1974

A Euan Lloyd Production. A MacLean and Co. Film. *Producer:* Euan Lloyd. *Director:* Ken Annakin. *Script:* Jack Davies. *Camera:* John Cabrera. *Production designer:* Herbert Smith. *Art:* Tony Reading, Peter Scharff. *Music:* Roy Budd. *Editor:* Alan Pattillo. *Running time:* 100 minutes. Technicolor.

CAST

David Niven . . . . *Bradbury*
Toshiro Mifune . . . . *Kagoyama*
Hardy Kruger . . . . *Muller*
Ando . . . . *Koichi*
Ivan Desny . . . . *Foreign Minister*
Irene Tsu . . . . *Talah*
Ronald Fraser . . . . *Forster*
Miike Taka . . . . *Mme Kagoyama*
Jeff Corey . . . . *Mr. King*
Patricia Donahue . . . . . . *Mrs. King*
Kurt Christian . . . . *Harok*
Jeanine Siniscal . . . . *Foreign Minister's Girl*

STORY

English teacher Walter Bradbury arrives in Kulagong, an island state of uncertain location but vaguely in the Pacific, to act as tutor to Koichi, 11-year-old son of the Japanese ambassador.

Bradbury, even in late middle-age, retains an impressive soldierly manner which adds credibility to the stories of his stirring military past with which he regales Koichi as he parades around with his heavy stick and damaged leg, suffered of course upon some past heroic occasion.

When urban guerillas attempt the assassination of the local foreign secretary at a Japanese Embassy party, Bradbury, quite by accident, foils the plot.

This action, naturally, enhances his gallant reputation. But the situation changes when the same guerilla group, headed by gun girl Talah, kidnaps Koichi and his tutor to attract attention to the fate of their jailed comrades.

Imprisoned by the guerillas Koichi looks to Bradbury

As Mr. Bradbury, a man who compensates for a colourless life by inventing an exciting and heroic past. (With Ando and Toshiro Mifune.)

The face of despair. The accumulated skills of nearly forty years in pictures went into the creation of this touching portrait.

to find an instant way out. Bradbury, whose tales of daring were all imaginary, collapses into his customary state of timidity. The pair wait while their captors negotiate their release with the government. But the government refuse to free the imprisoned revolutionaries.

Bradbury, at last, makes a successful effort to escape with Koichi and a chase over the exotic but unkindly countryside begins. Koichi's anxious father is not put at ease when Gunther Muller, a German TV reporter, uncharitably reveals that Bradbury's courageous past is just a fraud.

As the guerillas close in Bradbury is shot in the leg but does not give up. The timely arrival of a government helicopter save the pair and disposes of the guerillas.

Bradbury, at the conclusion of the one true heroic episode of his life, confesses his deception to Kagoyama and prepares to leave. But the ambassador assures him that his job is safe.

NOTES

This provided Niven with his best opportunity since *Separate Tables,* although it is not the similarities but the intriguing differences in the performances of kindred characters that attract the attention. The Major in *Separate Tables* was seedy and bogus. Poor Mr. Bradbury is bogus but he's never seedy. In *Separate Tables* author Terence Rattigan provided the actor with more useful footholds than Jack

Davies does in *Paper Tiger* and Bradbury is even more a piece of character creation by David Niven than was the case with his Major.

Unfortunately as a film *Paper Tiger* is not in the same class, being a straightforward piece of hokum adventure with what ought to be clearly defined goodies and badies and an agreeable 100 minutes to enjoy right triumphing over wrong.

The film, clearly, belongs in the setting of a South American republic but instead pops up in some curiously anonymous island in the Pacific packed with so many different nationalities in leading parts that the spectators become seriously disorientated.

This may have been due to the state of the British film industry at the time, where so many around-the-world guarantees were required before the money was forthcoming that the finished product almost demands dialogue in Esperanto.

In this sort of film the audience needs to know exactly where it stands and precisely whom to boo. Here the forces of good seem an unsavoury lot and the villains not unsympathetic; a creditable injection of truth, but in this sort of outdoor adventure yarn harsh reality is a disconcerting intruder. When in the finale the terrorists are summarily eliminated in the expected fashion, as the expendable bit players and extras they are, the more sensitive are likely to feel a twinge in the gut that mixes uneasily with a packet of pop-corn. This may seem, as some critics suggested, to leave Niven, once again, doing nothing

With Hardy Kruger.

more than a glorious shoring-up job, but against all the bangs and gaudy back drops he commands attention with his richest and most arresting performance for many years.

David Niven saw this film as a family show and hoped it would compete with the reigning disaster films such as *The Towering Inferno*.

The popular paper critics decided he had succeeded. 'Enjoyable piece of family entertainment,' said *The Sun*. 'I see the film being just as popular with kids as their parents,' said the *Daily Express*. 'A film for the whole family to enjoy,' echoed the *Daily Mirror*.

Margaret Hinxman in the *Daily Mail* was less charmed by the film and its principal character but observed: 'Niven's elegance and style make you feel the character is not nonsense, but a man at odds with a conscience the existence of which he had long since forgotten.' And she describes him in conclusion as the sort of man 'who can make any old film look like a priceless jewel'.

The men from the quality press seemed to move in with rather weightier engines of war than such a modest adversary deserved. Tom Hutchinson of the *Sunday Telegraph*, nevertheless, was enthusiastic about the star. 'What saves it all from absolute tepidity is David Niven's portrayal as Bradbury with a quotation for every situation and an excuse for every possible danger. The wary eye beneath the forehead's corrugations tells us the man has lived life at second-hand but would hate to be thought as second-rate. It is a satisfying example of combined star-quality and acting skill.'

'He really is a master of his craft,' said the *Spectator*.

'David Niven snuggles happily into his character,' said *The Times*.

The *Financial Times* found the film 'distinctly pernicious' and observed that David Niven 'is well tried at propping up such rickety vehicles'.

Patrick Gibbs in the *Daily Telegraph*, after dismissing the film, revealed that he was not happy with the Niven performance '... I was left feeling strongly that of all the cards Mr. Niven holds, pathos is not one of them.'

Russell Davies of the *Observer* was sour about the whole operation. 'Anyone who wishes to know why our film industry has lost its self-respect should certainly see *Paper Tiger*,' he rumbled. And dealt with the star thus: 'David Niven's recent book has saved him from relegation to the battered figurine department, making his shabby-genteel presence about as well known now as it ever has been.' If that is intended as a compliment it is about as welcome as the attentions of a passing mugger. If intended as a criticism it seems extraordinarily inept in view of the Niven acting record, and so the words must be treated as an expression of the critic's general sense of pique.

Again we see a general concensus of critical opinion

Hardy Kruger, Toshiro Mifune, David Niven and Ivan Desny.

that Niven, while maintaining his record of fine performances, has missed the sort of film that would give him an adequate setting; opinion that has sounded like a knell throughout his career.

This whole, sad situation was summed up by Dilys Powell in her review in the *Sunday Times*. 'David Niven plays with his unfailing elegance and that touch of pathos which is his especial gift . . . I wish only that someone could find the perfect role for Mr.

Niven. A Dickens character, perhaps? Something out of Thackeray or Meredith. I don't know. I know only that I long to see him recapturing and enlarging the qualities I saw in his tiny role in *Lady L*.

'He is an actor far more delicate, far more easily damaged by wrong treatment in the medium than his insouciant air might suggest. I can't help feeling that, lying around somewhere, there is a small master-piece for David Niven.'

FILMS
FOR
TELEVISION

The attitude of Hollywood to the TV world was one of bitter hostility and this helped to launch Dick Powell's Four Star Playhouse into almost inevitable success. He formed the company, with Niven and Charles Boyer as partners, to produce films for TV and persuade as many star chums to appear in them as possible.

The one thing the men of TV wanted badly and couldn't get was a few genuine film stars, most of whom were too scared of incurring the wrath of their bosses by deserting to the enemy.

Of course, the sort of material Four Star Playhouse turned out was calculated to drive more people into the cinema than it was ever likely to drive out but the film men, convinced that TV was stealing their patrons, were in no mood for fancy thinking. The star system still dominated and film producers were convinced that those who held the big names held the power.

It was not until the series *The Rogues* that Niven became involved in a TV production that even faintly aspired to the style and polish to be found in the cinema.

Dick Powell was the organising genius, Charles Boyer a fairly silent partner, and Niven, who makes no claim to great business flair, was a sort of goodwill man; another area in which he could exploit his charm and diplomacy. It put him, however, right in the hot-seat as far as the film companies were concerned. But as he was in trouble with the film companies at this time in any case (1952) he reckoned he had little to lose.

Ironically, if Four Star made no great contribution to the furtherance of TV art it produced and fed to the film business some useful future attractions, including Steve MacQueen.

Compared with some of his contemporaries, such as Glenn Ford, Shirley MacLaine, James Stewart and Henry Fonda, Niven, as actor, never more than flirted with the small screen.

253

The Rogues

DAVID NIVEN / CHARLES BOYER / GIG YOUNG

CO-STARRING

ROBERT COOTE / GLADYS COOPER

The masters of
con and charm
pull another
masterful caper

GUEST STARS INCLUDE: EDDIE ALBERT, BRODERICK CRAWFORD, HELMUT DANTINE, HOWARD DUFF, JAMES GREGORY, DIANA HYLAND, IDA LUPINO, ELSA MARTINELLI, WALTER MATTHAU AND DARREN McGAVIN.

254

Two scenes from *The Rogues.*

Niven the director: with James Whitmore on the set of *Wayfarers.*

ADDENDUM

At the time of going to press, David Niven has just completed a new film for the Disney Studios.

NO DEPOSIT, NO RETURN
(Shooting title: Double Trouble)

A Walt Disney Production. *Producers*: Ron Miller, Joseph McEveety. *Director:* Norman Tokar. *Script:* Arthur Alsberg and Don Nelson—*from the story by* Joseph McEveety. Technicolor.

CAST

David Niven. . . . .*J. W. Osborne*
Barbara Felden . . . . *Carolyn Osborne*
Kim Richards. . . . .*Tracy Osborne*
Brad Savage. . . . . *Jay Osborne*
Darren McGavin. . . . . *Duke Mayfield*
Don Knotts . . . . *Bert Delaney*
Vic Tayback. . . . . *Big Joe Adamo*

STORY

Eleven-year-old Tracy Osborne and her nine-year-old brother Jay are at loose ends during their Easter vacation. Their widowed mother Carolyn is in Hong Kong on business and they are being sent to Los Angeles to visit their wealthy grandfather, J. W. Osborne. He isn't looking forward to that, and neither are they. After a commotion at the airport on their arrival, J.W. sees his grandchildren off in a cab with two rusty safebreakers, Duke Mayfield and Bert Delaney. The kids talk themselves into holing up with Duke and Bert who are trying to pull one last caper to pay off a debt they owe to Big Joe Adamo. J.W. feels that a touch of adventure might be good for the runaways and secretly has them watched for their protection, but Tracy launches a plan to raise money for Duke and Bert as well as air fare to Hong Kong for herself and Jay. She mails a note to grandpa saying that she and her brother have been kidnapped and are being held for ransom. Amused by the ploy, J.W. declines to pay off. The story develops with the police and Big Joe becoming involved in the 'kidnapping' and

J.W. trying to retrieve the kids when their mother suddenly arrives home. Throughout the ensuing uproar, Tracy and Jay stay one step ahead of everybody, but end up locked in their grandfather's airtight walk-in safe in his mansion with only 30 minutes left before they will suffocate. It is left to Duke, sorely out of practice and with police eyes on him, to crack the safe and rescue the kids in the nick of time. All ends well, with Duke and Bert promising to go straight and J.W. taking the whole gang under his wing as one big happy family.

David Niven is currently working on a new film in Hollywood, **DEATH BY MURDER,** a comedy thriller written by Neil Simon and co-starring Maggie Smith, Alec Guinness, Peter Sellers, Peter Falk and also Truman Capote. A Ray Star Production.